Icarus World Issues Series

Coming of Age
The Art of Growing Up

Series Editors, Roger Rosen and Patra McSharry Sevastiades

D0609000

THE ROSEN PUBLISHING GROUP, INC.
NEW YORK

Published in 1994 by The Rosen Publishing Group, Inc.
29 E. 21st Street, New York, NY 10010

"Ute Creek Pass" Copyright © 1992 by Bruce Ducker.
"Eagles" is excerpted with permission of Uitgeverij De Geus from *De adelaars* by Kader Abdolah. Originally published as "De adelaars" by Uitgeverij De Geus. Copyright © 1993 by Uitgeverij De Geus bv, Amsterdam. Publication of "Eagles" was made possible in part by financial support from the Foundation for the Production and Translation of Dutch Literature.
"Ramona" Copyright © 1994 by Nicole Cooley.
"A Great Day of Accounting" Copyright © 1994 by Gerald Hadden.
"Romania's Children of the Street" is excerpted with permission of ANAKO Editions from *Roumanie: Les gamins du pavé* by Gérard Milhès and Hien Lam Duc, copyright © 1993 by ANAKO Editions, and *Graines d'Hommes*, edited by Patrick Bernard, copyright © 1992 by ANAKO Editions, Xonrupt-Longemer.
"Letters of the Sun, Letters of the Moon" is excerpted with permission of The Institute for the Translation of Hebrew Literature from *Letters of the Sun, Letters of the Moon* by Itamar Levy, published by Keter Publishing House Jerusalem Ltd. Translation copyright © 1994 by The Institute for the Translation of Hebrew Literature, Ramat Gan.
"A Little Piece of Lost Time" is excerpted with permission of the author. Originally published as "Las ortigas," "El barro," and "Cementerios de mariposas" in *El río* by Edicions Destino SA, Barcelona. Copyright © 1963 by Ana Maria Matute.
"Goodbye, Mother" is excerpted with permission of the author. Originally published as "Ate logo, mamãe" in the collection *O Moderno Conto Brasileiro*, edited by João Antonio, by Editora Civilizacão Brasileira, SA, Rio de Janeiro. Copyright © 1980 by Wander Piroli.
"Sugarplum Fairy" Copyright © 1994 by Sandra Tsing Loh.
"Ikop Mbog" Copyright © 1994 by Nouk Bassomb.
"A Miracle" is excerpted with permission of Harcourt Brace from *Moving House and Other Stories* by Pawel Huelle, to be published in February 1995 by Harcourt Brace & Co., Inc., New York. Originally published in 1991 as *Opowiadania na czas przeprowadzki* by Puls Publications Ltd., London.
"Aman" is excerpted with permission of Pantheon Books from the book *Aman: The Story of a Somali Girl*, to be published in September by Pantheon Books, A Division of Random House, Inc., New York. Text copyright © 1994 by Aman and the Estate of Virginia Lee Barnes. Foreword and Afterword copyright © 1994 by Janice Boddy .

First Edition

Library of Congress Cataloging-in-Publication Data

Coming of age : the art of growing up. -- 1st ed.
    p. cm. -- (Icarus world issues series)
Edited by Roger Rosen and Patra McSharry Sevastiades.
Includes bibliographical references and index.
Summary: A collection of fictional and non-fictional stories and essays by a variety of authors dealing with the experience of becoming an adult.
    ISBN 0-8239-1805-X. -- ISBN 0-8239-1806-8
    1. Youth--Literary collections.   [1. Youth--Literary collections.]   I. Rosen, Roger.   II. Sevastiades, Patra McSharry. III. Series.
PZ5.C7437   1994
808.8 ' 0352055--dc20   94-27347
                                                                     CIP
                                                                      AC

Manufactured in the United States of America

Contents

Introduction

The eminent English Victorian art critic John Ruskin called Michelanglo's "David" a "hobbledehoy," a gawky adolescent. Most people who pay homage to this statue as a Renaissance icon see white marble and think classical proportions, man as the measure of all things, and Praxitelean principles. But such folk are on a whirlwind grand tour and not looking too closely. What Ruskin saw, and what is there for all to see, are the disproportionately large hands, the clodhopper feet, and the painfully oversized head. If Michelangelo had heard of photorealism, David would surely have had a face full of pimples. If David were to speak, his voice would crack. It's disorienting to think of the slayer of Goliath and the future king of Israel in this light, but then all greatness has not only a small beginning but a midway chrysalis, an awkward and uncomfortable transformational stage.

David, then, is the epitome of the male adolescent. He is instantly recognizable by his slingshot—an iconography worthy of the boyish imaginings of a Spielberg or a Lucas. You needn't have one of their plot lines or a spell on a psychiatrist's couch—whether Freudian or Jungian—to read Goliath as the "Father." Just consider his size and the threat.

In psychic terms every youth must "kill" his parents; that is, break his dependent relationship with them. Without this violence it is impossible to reach the next stage of development, the entry into adulthood. Nowadays, of course, we have become so depraved, so blind to the meaning of our own symbols, so ensnared in a prolonged psychic childhood—dependent and codependent—that psychic transformations don't take place. In their stead we have actual parent killers in the Menendez brothers mode, a Beverly Hills 123 quick pull of the trigger and grab at the booty. David would have been appalled.

Why so much speculation on the meaning of young David? Ultimately one can't help wondering whether coming of age has radically changed since biblical times. Clearly what was experienced by David was different from the world perceived by a young Bathsheba. What of the initiation of women into the adult mysteries? The Old Testament might not have considered the subject worthy of attention but we most certainly do. Hence our latest volume "Coming of Age: The Art of Growing Up." For surely the process of maturation is as fraught with perils, challenges, and triumphs as Michelangelo's own endeavor. To grow up well is indeed an art. In the fifteenth volume of *Icarus*, we offer you the mad explosion of hormones, the ache of growing bones, the ham-fisted attempts at savoir faire, the unconscious examples of achingly perfect grace. So join us as we follow Cameroonian author Nouk Bassomb in the mystical path of Bassa initiation, and take ballet lessons with Janine at the Mahri School of Dance in California, and live rough with thousands of Romanian children who suffer from Ceausescu's profligacy. In each offering, you will find the chrysalis torn open to reveal all that was and all that might be. Here it comes to pass.

Roger Rosen, Editor

SUGARPLUM FAIRY

SANDRA TSING LOH

Sandra Tsing Loh was born in Newport Beach, California. She earned a bachelor's degree in physics from the California Institute of Technology and a master's degree in English literature from the University of Southern California.

Ms. Loh is a free-lance writer whose work has appeared in *Glamour, Mademoiselle,* and the *Los Angeles Times,* among other publications. She has been a guest columnist for the *Los Angeles Times Magazine* and writes a monthly column for *Buzz* magazine.

In addition, Ms. Loh is a pianist who performs music in a witty theatrical fashion. "Spontaneous Demographics," the performance that opened the Fringe Festival/LA in 1987, featured Ms. Loh playing a piano concert for the commuters locked in rush-hour traffic on the Harbor Freeway. Ms. Loh's repertoire also feaures solo musical and theatrical performances, including the performance monologue "My Father's Chinese Wives." Her solo piano album, "Pianovision," was released in 1992.

Ms. Loh lives in Van Nuys, California.

All I know is, one October night in 1976 we ceased being Ballet people and became Nutcracker people.

It had been a day like any other day. My older sister Kaitlin and I had eaten the same after-school snacks (Muenster on pumpernickel, V-8, apple). We had worn our Thursday leotards (she: navy and white V-neck, me: orange with skater's skirt). We had attended our usual afternoon classes at the Mahri School of Dance (Kaitlin: Ballet 3 in the big studio, me: Ballet 2 in the little).

Now, at 7:35 p.m., my mother was driving us home in the same Ford Fairmont. And she was launching into her usual speech.

"Attack!" my mother cried out in despair, as we sat under the red glare of the stoplight. This was to Kaitlin, of course, who always sat in the front seat, hunched and sullen in her parka. At sixteen, Kaitlin was "the brilliant one"—and therefore the one who most often disappointed. I always rode home in the darkness and quiet of the back seat, enjoying Vanilla Finger cookies, far from achievement and its many complications.

"That's what your fouetté needs! Attack!" my mother insisted, her eyes wild and worried behind their large round glasses. "What is wrong with you? You are like a noodle. Lifeless." My mother slumped forward over the steering wheel, her eyes shut, mouth dropped open, to illustrate.

Kaitlin's eyes narrowed. She set her jaw and turned away to stare at the Jack in the Box, which blazed in the darkness like a hallucination. Her words were small, tight. "My hamstring . . . was sore."

"Always with the hamstring!" My mother shook her head violently. "How many more times are you going to go on about this hamstring?"

There was a pause. The truth was, Kaitlin had been

milking the hamstring thing too long. But why? Why the excuses? I sighed. If I were allowed to sit in the front seat on the way home, in the hot seat, I would never give my mother the lip Kaitlin did. I would have taken that advice and applied it!

But of course, it wasn't my place to say. "The fouetté is certainly a difficult movement," was what I now diplomatically put forth, leaning in from my back-seat post. "Although I feel that my own turns are going well enough in Ballet 2, I can tell that in Ballet 3 things will be quite—"

"Sometimes I wonder with you, Kaitlin," my mother continued, switching lanes, sorrowful. A softer tone was creeping into her voice, something intimate. "Do you even want these lessons? We can stop if you want. Heaven knows it's not cheap. If ballet is just a big chore, you should let me know. If getting picked by Irina Lichinskaya to dance in 'The Nutcracker' is not important to you . . ." she let the words hang in the air.

The skin prickled on the back of my neck. I felt a thrill and a pang of jealousy at the same time. Irina Lichinskaya was the balletmistress of the Los Angeles Junior Ballet. Word had it that Irina had defected from the Bolshoi in the '50's, had briefly married a duke, had lived in Monte Carlo for ten years. She was a legendary figure, a starmaker, with connections to John Clifford and the ABT. She was the sort of person who could take an average ballet student living an average life at the average Mahri School of Dance and lift her up to . . . ?

As for "The Nutcracker"—well, this was the most glittering spectacle one could imagine. The Los Angeles Junior Ballet's "Nutcracker," which our family had gone to see three years in a row, was always held in the Wilshire Theater, a veritable palace of columns and balustrades, its proscenium decorated with red velvet curtains, painted cherubs, and gold tassels. In the pit was a real orchestra, the men and women all in black tie, holding real oboes and violins.

And when the curtain lifted? This was a land I had seen only in Walt Disney Specials: glowing candelabra, twisting candy canes, bejeweled trees, dancing bears, mechanical dolls, gingerbread houses, flying walnut boats. Most amazing of all, however, was that girls my age—looking impressively adult in full costume and makeup, their hair curled and sprayed—were threading their way through this magical scenery, their faces warmed by the glow of the footlights. They were the special girls, the Los Angeles Junior Ballet girls. The large and worshipful audience chuckled and sighed and broke into applause.

"If getting picked by Irina Lichinskaya for 'The Nutcracker' isn't important to you," my mother continued, clicking her blinker off, guileless, "we don't have to go any more, ever again. I certainly won't be the one to push you. I wouldn't even want to drive you to class that day if your heart wasn't in it. I might just stay home myself that day, if that's what you want."

Kaitlin turned back toward my mother. I could see my sister's pale face, illuminated by the passing street lamps. Bulky parka or no, she always had a certain nobility when her dark hair was up in a bun, like Grace Kelly. She closed her almond-shaped eyes as though nauseated by the whole topic.

"No, it's fine," Kaitlin said through her teeth, a prisoner beaten into unwanted confession. "I *will* try to . . . work . . . on . . . the fouettés." Before she turned away again, a scowl twisted across her face, as though to register how little she really cared about any of this.

Kaitlin in "The Nutcracker"? Ha. I felt sour with the injustice of it. Kaitlin would probably scowl as she hopped her way across the stage, much as she did in Ballet 3. Afterward she would complain about her hamstring.

My mother, however, chose not to see the scowl. She ended the conversation by giving a curt nod of approval.

"What a workout we had in Ballet 2 today!" I exclaimed, pressing my hands against the back of my mother's seat, half-willing her to turn around and look at me. "Those leaps we did—I practically broke into a sweat! Did you see, Mama? Real sweat!"

Feeling generous, my mother glanced over her shoulder and tossed me a bone. Her evaluations of my performance were always vague, complimentary, and delivered in an oddly hearty tone. "And you, Janine! Hey! Sure! Showing some improvement, I think!"

I certainly didn't think I was a bad dancer. Only three years younger than Kaitlin, I had been studying almost as long as she had. I was a pretty good jumper and could do the split.

That's right—the split. I could sink all the way down. Well, almost all the way down; in truth, I had to cheat a little to the right to get my hips to sit on the floor. But when you looked in the mirror, you saw a person who was doing the split. No doubt about it. I could sit there for five minutes without too much bouncing. I imagined Irina Lichinskaya, elegant in pearls, black cocktail dress, and heels, clicking by, tapping a cigarette holder toward me. "I'll take this one," she'd say. "Look: She can do the split."

Secretly I felt that, given the opportunity to perform in "The Nutcracker," I might even turn out to be the real Ballet person in the family. Because the fact was, I adored ballet much more than Kaitlin did. That is, I loved what I understood to be the true "dance" part of it—the whirling about the room, the other dancers and the wall of mirrors spinning around you, kaleidoscopic, the wind fluttering by, the music surging forward, you following its lead. It was intoxicating. I would emerge from ballet class exhilarated and a bit dizzy.

I loved the battered Mahri School of Dance, the way it looked. I loved the wooden walls, the potted plants, and the shiny black upright piano. I loved the green benches in the hall and the tattered poster of pink satin point shoes tacked up in the bathroom. "Ballet . . ." it said, "is Inspiration."

I loved Mahri herself. Mahri was a plump, cheerful, elderly Englishwoman who resembled something from Beatrix Potter. She had a cap of silver hair and was given to wearing odd costumes whose origins lay somewhere between the worlds of the dance and the tea party—beige woolen vests and bell-bottoms, for instance, with long strands of pearls and little white dance slippers. Occasionally a daisy (never explained) appeared behind Mahri's ear.

Forgiveness and warmth flowed from Mahri. She was happy just to see her "gehls," as she called us, no matter what their state. Even her occasional admonitions were loving. "We've had quite a bit of porridge this week, haven't we?" she might say, tapping her cane gently on my stomach. But then she'd move in to massage my shoulder, as one would a dumb but loyal workhorse. "All right, then. Tuck in," she'd murmur, closing her eyes, taking a deep breath herself, "Fwhhhhhp!" The eyes would open. The tip of her finger would light under my chin, tilt it up a centimeter. That was all it took. I was transformed from a mere thirteen-year-old girl into a ballerina. "Beautiful. Beautiful."

What Kaitlin had going for her, as far as I could see, was perfect form. First position, passé, relevée, attitude, arabesque: Her movements were neat, tidy. Any bystander could tell that she was pleased with her ballet. But in her own private way, it was not as though this pleasure were something she felt compelled to share with the world. There was more of a cool quality, a precise quality—as if she were some type of sleek engine, as if she were saying, "So, all right. There isn't a bad angle on me."

She was aloof. (That word intrigued me: "aloof." "Aloof," I would sometimes say to myself, winging out one arm and then dropping it as though I just didn't care.)

In ballet, as in everything, she was curiously removed from the world. But not hostile to it—although I was but a spot in her universe, for instance, I wasn't a black spot. Kaitlin would give me an occasional nod as I came panting out of Ballet 2. "You worked today," she'd say, as though this were some cryptic measure of worth.

Before class, other girls would throw themselves into punishing stretching exercises, practice triple pirouettes, or engage in other attention-getting ploys. Not Kaitlin. Kaitlin would stand in front of the mirror and engage in a simple ritual of form. It was almost mathematical. She would hold her stick-thin arms before her in a circle, and then move them out. In . . . and then out. In . . . and then out. It was as though this were the only tiny vanity she would afford herself.

Very occasionally, with her arms still out, Kaitlin would pivot in order to appreciate the side view of herself. One arm still up, she'd liberate the other for a quick moment to run her hand down her flat belly. A dramatic sigh would follow. What did this sigh mean? Was she thinking about the vagaries of Ballet 3 (which I had been told was much harder than Ballet 2)? Was she thinking of high school and its (apparently) many calculus tests? There was a certain fascinating 11th-grade world-weariness to it all. After a moment, Kaitlin would give a quick nod and shake her skinny arms out, as if suddenly bored.

"Did you see Darlene Kester's hair?" my mother laughed, her eyes sparkling, vivid, hard, with the absurdity of it. It was exactly one week before the audition: Nerves were on edge at the Mahri School of Dance.

"Cheryl Tiegs she's not," Kaitlin assented as she shrugged out of her parka and into her ballet slippers. "Although she may think she is. Where Darlene really belongs is Hollywood, not in a ballet class."

Indeed, Darlene Kester's hair was quite a sight.

Overnight, her bun had gone from mousy brunette to streaky blonde. Not only that: If you looked closely, it appeared that a thin line of blue pencil and shadow had been applied over each eye. So she was wearing makeup too! Darlene's savvy transformation was like the first hat thrown into the ring, if you will, the first salvo of battle.

"Look at her mother, though. Is it any wonder?" confided Mrs. Anderson to Mama. Mrs. Anderson's daughter was pudgy, red-haired Arlette. Within the "Nutcracker" universe, Arlette was not a threat; therefore my mother regarded Mrs. Anderson as a kind of comrade-in-arms. Arlette had braces and was ravaged by acne. Literally ravaged. Her class photo that year showed her with eyes closed, lips half-parted, as if exhausted with herself. ("But she has nice arches," my mother would always point out charitably. "She has a nice point. Mein Gott," she'd finish finally, shaking her head. "Poor Arlette!")

"What of her mother?" my mother wanted to know.

"She just got divorced from that dentist—you know, Bud Kester, of Kester Dentistry on 24th Street?" Mrs. Anderson's expression was baleful. My mother leaned closer. "I hate to say it," Mrs. Anderson continued, "but word has it that Mrs. Kester . . . likes her liquor."

"What a shame," replied my mother, making a grave face. Her voice shivered with sympathy. "I had wondered. Of course, it's tough being a woman by yourself. Very tough. I should know. But how we each deal with it is a different matter. Sometimes when Mrs. Kester drops Darlene off for the five o'clock pointe class—in that Cadillac—she's a bit giddy, if you know what I mean."

"No supervision," Mrs. Anderson murmured as her gaze followed Darlene, who at that moment was warming up . . . by doing piqué turns energetically across the room. When Darlene reached the corner, she practically collided with my sister, who was grimly doing her preclass arm thing. Kaitlin simply took a step to the side and continued, not even glancing in Darlene's direction. But her scowl seemed to deepen. "No supervision whatsoever," Mrs. Anderson repeated. "It's really quite sad."

"That hair looks awful. Like a floozy. Anyway, I'm not sure that kind of thing counts with Irina Lichinskaya."

"Not at all," Mrs. Anderson agreed. "In fact, Darlene's hair will probably hurt her chances."

"Well," my mother put up her hands, as though to distance herself from the situation. "It's a big, big world. There's room for everybody, I suppose. Blond hair or no hair: It takes all kinds!"

It was all kinds, all right, that showed up the following Thursday for Irina Lichinskaya's much-anticipated visit. At the last moment, it was announced that Ballet 2 students would be allowed to attend the audition as well as Ballet 3. As a result, sixty girls—practically every living Mahri student—were packed into the big studio. All the usual suspects were there—Darlene Kester, of course, Arlette Anderson (all in white, unfortunately, not a slimming color), the Todesco twins, little Martha Heninger.

The excitement was pitched to hysteria. Even the accessories were hysterical: the odd, never-before-seen flowers poked into buns, the brand-new Capezio dance skirts, and even the borrowed-from-Mom flashy earrings. One girl had miniature gold toe shoes hanging from her ears.

"She's here!" someone called out.

In the tiny visitor's area, people were scattering in Irina Lichinskaya's path. Mothers' hands were aflutter. The Mahri School of Dance receptionist and interns were running forward with pitcher of water and drinking glasses, clearing a bench, closing blinds behind her to remove potential glare. Then opening them. Then closing them. This way gave more light. But that way blocked the heat. Which way?

As the throng parted, Irina emerged.

"Boy," whispered Kaitlin, "that woman has had a rough life!"

Well into her sixties, Irina Lichinskaya, professional star-maker, stood no more than five foot two. She had lank, jet-black, dyed hair cut into a girlish pageboy. Her face was flushed, and she had one rheumy eye; bright red lipstick slashed across her mouth. She wore a black wool dress, an oddly mannish trench coat, and little black boots. In contrast to Mahri's refined tea-party appearance, Irina looked rather like a bag lady.

Irina leaned shakily over the wooden rail of the visitor's area and waved at the crowd.

"Hyello, leddies!" she called out in a raspy voice. "Jast don't mind me. Jast go forss as zough I am note here!"

Nervous tittering arose from the Mahri School of Dance hopefuls. For a moment, it was as though we were all going to break into spontaneous applause at this odd announcement.

"Leddies? May I introdoose Corinna?" Irina led a rail-thin, thirtyish, fabulous-looking brunette out by the hand. "She will be lidding your egsercises today." Corinna, in black pedal pushers, a kind of white, Audrey Hepburn blouse tied at the waist, and amber knob earrings, her short glossy hair swept back in a wide cream headband, nodded curtly to us.

"Look at that number," Kaitlin murmured. "She's not going to stick around doing Irina's dirty work for long. I give her six months and she's history."

"We are vair vair lacky that Corinna has tecken time out of hair busy schidule to cam today! *Vair vair* lacky." Corinna looked back at Irina, who still clutched her hand. Some undecipherable look passed between them. Irina leaned forward and whispered something in her ear.

Corinna shook her hair out and gave a short sardonic laugh. We Mahri School of Dance hopefuls smiled expectantly, exchanging glances, wondering if we should laugh too.

The answer was no. Corinna immediately turned and, without expression, began moving her arms in a decisive motion as she cut through the crowd toward the mirror.

"And a one and two. And a one and two . . . " You followed this woman, no matter what. Mesmerized and a bit frightened, we all fell into step behind her.

Corinna was not terribly interested in the barre. She breezily led us through a handful of pliés and cambres. She pulled at her earlobes as though her fabulous earrings bothered her. She gave the shortest of stretch sections. We barely had time to settle into our splits before we were supposed to pop up again.

Vainly I looked after her as I sat in my patented split, hip tilted carefully to the right, with hardly any bouncing. Other girls around me groaned, shook out their legs. Still I sat. Where was the calling out of my name, the magical tap on my shoulder? I improvised a kind of wild port de bras to accentuate the effect.

But to no avail: Corinna was at the other end of the room having a glass of water. Putting it down, she touched the corner of her mouth as if to fix her lipstick. Then she abruptly waved at the pianist to conclude.

"And now," Corinna announced, facing us. "Come to the center. I will teach you steps from the Cechetti method."

I shot a startled glance at Kaitlin.

Nothing of the kind had ever been discussed in Ballet 2. We did the barre; we did a center adagio where we stood in one place and swung our arms lyrically about to Pachelbel's *Canon*; we did our waltz number; we ended with jumps, bounding up and down as though on a trampoline. That was it. What was the Cechetti method?

"And a one and a two?" Corinna said, as though asking some kind of deep metaphysical question, as she extended her right leg forward. "And a one and a two," she replied, as if that were the whole answer right there, doing a quick relevée on her left leg, closing and beating the right leg twice at the left knee, and then whipping it out to the side, her left leg spasming upward into another quick relevée before going into a deft 180-degree pivot.

A taut silence gripped the ragged semicircle of Mahri School of Dancers. No one so much as moved, but faces were turning pale. This wasn't dance, this was . . . algebra.

"Mark the steps," whispered Kaitlin, her eyes fixed on Corinna. It was the first ballet-oriented advice she had ever given me. It made me feel grave—that she was holding a door open, letting me glimpse all the grim complexities of her adult life. "Just remember to mark the steps. Do them along with her when she demonstrates. Mark . . . the . . . steps," Kaitlin hissed one final time, as though pressing a sacred talisman upon me.

"All right?" Corinna asked. "In groups of eight, then."

The pianist began the intro, and eight stalwart Ballet 3 students stepped forward. Included was blond Darlene, in a brand-new fuchsia Danskin leotard she had purchased specially for the occasion. Much good would it do her now.

Um pa pa, um pa pa, um pa pa, um pa pa . . .

You could feel an audible breath . . .

And then seven girls plunged fatally off in different directions, soldiers falling before the enemy. The Cechetti method had slain them. But one person stood fast. Kaitlin. Yes. There she stood in the center, as steely as a weathervane, as precise as a clock. Gone was the hamstring problem, the scowl. Her face was eerily calm, as though in repose. But below the neck, what movement. Unbelievably, she was beating the right leg at the left knee, whipping it outward, doing a quick relevée with the left and then deftly moving into the pivot . . . just like Corinna. There wasn't a trace of hesitation, not the barest hop.

As Irina Lichinskaya and the entire Mahri School of Dance crowd (the sixty students, the anxious mothers) watched, Kaitlin blazed with the complete hauteur of her perfect form. In all her frosty glory, Kaitlin was the beam of a lighthouse glimpsed above a stormy sea. In that moment, I saw with startling clarity that for all my gusto and my half-split, I couldn't do *that*. I would never be able to grasp *that*. And *that* was ballet—*that* was the elusive thing that made one girl stand out from one hundred.

And all my girlish fantasies—that I was good at ballet, that people were admiring me as I hurtled across the room, that I had something uniquely "extra," that I might even, perhaps, star in "The Nutcracker"—faded away. Until this point in my life, I had had no idea that I *wasn't* talented—but now I looked into the very Face of Talent. So this was what Talent looked like.

I had never before in my thirteen years been able to consider Talent so abstractly, so objectively. In her keen sixteen-year-old sense, Kaitlin understood every tiny part of her body and how it fit together. Her ballet was not about flinging oneself into the passion of the moment, but about a series of precise, perfectly honed images. Click click click. It was not about sloppy adolescent enthusiasm, but perfect clarity. In one breath, I saw my sister sail away on that big catamaran called Talent, leaving me far behind—tiny, shabby, lost on the gray shore.

"Sugarplum Fairy?" Corinna whispered to Irina. Irina said nothing, her bleary eyes fixed on my sister.

The question was not which key role to give to Kaitlin, it was how many. My mother related all this to us in a tumble, as she drove us home that night in the Ford Fairmont.

Irina Lichinskaya had initially thought Kaitlin might be good as the Spanish Princess; Corinna had felt they needed her more as a leader of the Merlitons—a tough dance with a lot of hopping en pointe. Or Snow Queen perhaps? Then again, the Flowers always needed a front-person, oh Lord, did they. In fact, Kaitlin could probably do all four roles, with plenty of time for a costume change. The Sugarplum Fairy, after all, was usually danced by one of the twenty-two-year-olds on leave from the lower ranks of the ABT. It was an advanced role, really, full of technical challenge.

On the other hand, it was the type of role that, if done well, could lead Kaitlin . . . to New York. In New York was Baryshnikov. In New York was the Lincoln Center. My mother went on and on, her voice soaring, cresting, swooping. "Baryshnikov," "Lincoln Center," "New York"—these were words that none had ever dared breathe before in the Fairmont. But now it was as though my mother were taking them out one by one and examining them and even claiming them. Kaitlin could make these wonders all hers too, it seemed, just by saying them aloud.

Kaitlin did not smile, but her face seemed to shine in the passing street lamps that night. New York, I thought in awe. New York. She was really that good. I had not seen it, not seen it at all. I had thought I was the one who was good. How pathetic, how awful, how wretched. I wanted to shrink away now and become invisible.

In short . . .

"How are Kaitlin's fouettés?" had been the blunt question put to my mother. "They're coming along very well, very well indeed," had been her bold reply.

Kaitlin's face contorted into a hideous mask. "Fouettés!" Kaitlin cried out in a kind of tragic half-shriek that was terrible to hear: "Oh noooooooooooo! You know that's the one thing I can't do! I always fall backward!"

But my mother had an answer for everything. A week ago Kaitlin had been a limp noodle: This week, she was the queen of balletdom, capable of anything.

"All you need," my mother broke in, her voice quiet, confident, jubilant, "is a little more attack. That's all. Just like I've been telling you. Look at Darlene Kester. We may laugh at Darlene's hair, and heaven knows she has the flattest feet in the world, but her turns . . . are not bad. When she does her fouettés, Darlene does have . . . a certain attack. See?"

My mother sat back from the steering wheel, pulling herself straight up like a top. She lifted a finger in front of her nose, and made a tight twirling motion with it. "And spot . . . and spot." She made the twirling motion again. "And spot . . . and spot." How did my mother know so much about ballet, anyway? As far as I know, she had never so much as eased her five foot eleven body into a leotard. If only she could stand in for us during these key moments, I thought, this would all be a lot easier.

"Why do I have to be the Sugarplum Fairy?" Kaitlin pleaded. "Why can't I just do the Spanish Dance? Why can't I just do the Merlitons? I can't do fouettés right even in class. How am I going to do them on stage before 500 people?"

"We'll work on it at home," my mother promised, "we'll do that spotting exercise in the kitchen. Every night."

"Oh noooooooooooo," Kaitlin repeated, a bit more listlessly. It was as though the magic that had come on so quickly had evaporated. All at once, with all that hair swept up, her furry parka fringed around her frail neck like a regal collar, my sixteen-year-old sister looked old and tired.

"Are you eating again, Janine?" my mother turned abruptly to look at me.

I felt my face go hot.

"Uh . . . yeah," I replied, putting my hand over my mouth, quickly swallowing my Vanilla Finger. What kind of a question was that? "Just . . . um, just a cookie. I—I just needed a pick-me-up." That was a phrase I had heard my mother use, her blanket word for the snacks she always had in her purse and in the car.

"Janine dear, you need to start thinking about just having a piece of fruit after class. You're getting to be a big girl, quite big. Poor Janine. Well, your grandmother always said you had good solid legs—legs that an empire could stand on."

"What?" I asked, confused. I was a "big girl"? Since when? I didn't recall ever being "big." In that instant, I saw a faint smile cross Kaitlin's face—as though my mother's comment had amused her, in spite of her general weariness. So this was a secret they shared between them, an awareness! Of my bigness.

But the smile faded, Kaitlin turning to my mother and murmuring words that were even more incredible: "This overeating thing. It's just a phase. Janine will grow out of it."

"What are you saying?" I cried. "That I'm . . . heavy?"

"Spot . . . and spot," my mother's voice came from the kitchen. "Spot . . . and spot." It was two weeks later. Kaitlin had been training with Corinna by day, drilling with my mother by night. Kaitlin's big rehearsal/fouetté showdown with Irina was tomorrow.

"It's no use," I could hear Kaitlin replying, weary.

"I know you can do it, Kaitlin. If you would just have a little more confidence in yourself. You need to believe in yourself. Spot . . . and spot. Spot . . . and spot."

I lounged in the darkness of the living room. I had snuck out a small jar of peanut butter from the pantry. I would plunge my forefinger into it, then lick it off. I had been doing this for twenty minutes. Plunge, lick. Plunge, lick. I had consumed half the jar and I felt sick. But what did it matter? I was fat. I was fat like Arlette Anderson: We were one and the same. Toadlike. Soon I would have terrible acne. I could see it coming.

On the bathroom scale, under the harsh glare of the fluorescents, I had discovered that I weighed 143 pounds. 143 pounds! It was like a weird dream. It couldn't be possible. Did my mother even weigh that much? I was enormous.

So that's why Mahri always said that thing about the porridge. Even Mahri, kind loving Mahri, knew. She had felt sorry for me. I was not "Beautiful, beautiful." How had this grotesque transformation happened? That's what the "Nutcracker" experience had brought to me. I would never again be able to enjoy a sandwich and wear shorts at the same time.

"Janine?"

I started. Pulled my sweatshirt over the peanut butter. Wheeled around in my armchair. But it was just Kaitlin. I shrugged. What did Kaitlin care if I was fat.

"Hel-lo," I replied. I curled up in a ball to make way for her to pass, found myself remaining there.

"I'm glad you get to be a Flower," Kaitlin sat down opposite, on the couch, in the darkness. Kaitlin's hips were slim. She never ate, never. "Are you excited?"

"Oh . . . I suppose so. There are, what—twenty-five of us? I just hope they find enough pink tulle in the city to cover us all." Arlette Anderson was a Flower too, and the Todesco twins. All the fat girls: To the last man, we had been jettisoned into the vegetable kingdom. In the hellish *bolge*, in the cruel Darwinian pecking order of "The Nutcracker," only the "Waltz of the Flowers," the lowest rung, would do for us. Any girl who could pull a pair of tights up over her hips could be a Flower.

Because the "Waltz of the Flowers" relied on easy effects, you could do with some gifted first-graders. Open the flowers. Close the flowers. Shake your hands like petals. Turn. That done, the Flowers' main job was to stand on stage in a semicircle and look on interestedly while our "ringer"—not a true Flower but a kind of mutant Turbo-"Rosette," played by none other than the vivacious Darlene Kester—piqué-turned about. With that famous *attack* of hers. All this on a slice of grapefruit and Tab.

"I'm going to be humiliated tomorrow," Kaitlin said suddenly.

"What?"

Her voice floated across the darkness at me like a strange fog. "No, it's true. I am." She turned to put her back against the arm of the couch. I could see her Grace Kelly-like profile perfectly silhouetted.

"Oh, I'm sure you'll get it," I mumbled, unsure.

"No," Kaitlin repeated, with perfect, calm conviction. She continued, as though discussing the results of an interesting experiment. "My spotting isn't that good. Not yet. I think it's because my weight is falling backward on the relevée. Our old teacher used to position us that way. It's something I have to relearn. But not in three weeks."

And she was right. After all, she was the genius. She *knew.*

In fact, in the years to come, Kaitlin would turn out to have been right about many things. Darlene Kester did belong in Hollywood: In 1985, Darlene would make a brief splash as an actress in an endlessly running Jiffy Pop commercial. Irina Lichinskaya's Junior Ballet would turn out to be small potatoes for fabulous Corinna, who'd move to New York to start her own clothing boutique. Word would have it that Corinna had been seen in close company with Martina Navratilova in Cannes one summer—never confirmed.

As for me, my hideous adolescent poundage, my ugliness, my toad-dom, would indeed turn out to be a phase. As would Arlette Anderson's. My sister foresaw that too. Although that sad heavy girl of thirteen was one I would always carry inside of me, even as I changed my clothes, my hairstyle, my diets.

But the one thing Kaitlin was wrong about was that she did not humiliate herself the next day. Far from it.

The pianist, Mrs. Consuela, began the Sugarplum Fairy intro just as planned. Um plum, um plum, um plum, um plum. Um plum, um plum, um plum, um plum . . .

On cue, Kaitlin whipped her right leg out and began the painful but impressive hopping-on-one-pointe sequence that opened the Sugarplum Fairy dance. She neatly ended the phrase with a deft skip-turn-plié, to murmurs of approval from the throng of watching students and mothers. "Thet's lovely, darling. Lovely," Irina called out, clapping her beringed, wrinkled hands.

Piqués done with her usual finicky neatness followed. More approval. Then two short stag leaps done with perfect landings. A general sigh. And then, as though buoyed by the music, it seemed, Kaitlin bouréed finally toward the center, the site of the dreaded fouetté sequence, like a lamb to slaughter . . .

But instead of stopping, pointing, plié-ing, and launching dutifully into her turns, that day Kaitlin kept bourée-ing. And bourée-ing. And bourée-ing. Her speed picked up, finally forcing her to break into a run.

"Dahling?" Irina called out, uncertainly. Mrs. Consuela looked nervously over her shoulder—but kept playing.

Because there was no stopping Kaitlin. Before the stunned crowd of mothers and students, Kaitlin began to run about the big studio. And run. (It was not unlike Giselle's mad scene, I'd realize later.) People instinctively stepped back, as one does when a bomb is about to go off. Kaitlin seemed to be shaking her head no, no, no. And then, giving one final, riveting leap, Kaitlin ran right out of the studio, down the stairs, out the door, left to the corner, and caught the bus home.

I myself didn't have the courage to run from "The Nutcracker." That wasn't what was written for me. I stayed, I did my three waltz steps, I was zipped into my huge pink costume, I ate my sandwiches. But what I did have, on the night of our opening, was a vision—a vision that glimmered beyond the flower corsages, the hairspray, the tiaras. Even within the clouds of my own misery, I had glimpsed that pure steely thing inside of Kaitlin. Call it character, call it stubbornness—and heaven knows my mother would call it many more things than that. Whatever it was, this pure steely thing got my respect.

This was the true revelation of my thirteenth year: that there was a kind of integrity that was invisible to the world. That there were acts of courage that reaped no earthly reward. That somewhere in the darkness of the audience, my sister sat, bearing her terrible burden, knowing all. Slowly I waltzed with my twenty-four compatriots—our hair curled, our faces powdered and rouged—in the glare of the footlights.

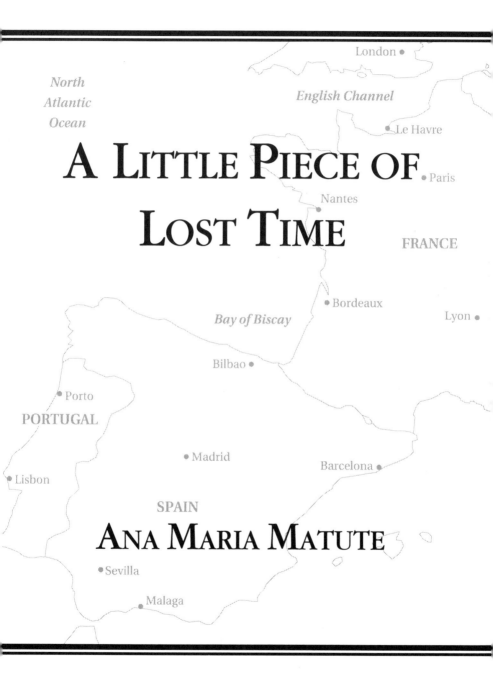

A LITTLE PIECE OF LOST TIME

ANA MARIA MATUTE

Ana Maria Matute was born in Barcelona. She is the author of twenty-seven books, including *The Stupid Children*, *First Memory*, and *The Dead Sons*. Her work has been translated into more than twenty languages.

Ms. Matute has received numerous literary awards, including the Café Gijón Prize in 1948, the Critics' Prize in 1958, the National Literature Prize in 1959, and the Fasthernath Prize in 1969. In 1984 she was awarded the National Prize in Children's Literature.

Ms. Matute has donated manuscripts of her works and other documents to the Ana Maria Matute Collection at Boston University, Massachusetts. She is a member of the Hispanic Society of America, and she is an honorary fellow of the America Association of Teachers of Spanish and Portuguese.

The following selection is excerpted from her collection *El río* (The River).

Nettles

I have forgotten most of the names of the flowers, plants, and fruits of the field. Not the names given to them by people who know, but the names we called them as children, the ones we learned from the other children of the village.

In those days we really understood the life of plants. Each of them had a life that was light and profound at the same time, a mysterious life. Lying among the brambles, we could almost breath the hidden essence of the earth. There were guileless plants, plants that were seething, sullen, friendly, evil, and venomous. We knew them all. The poppy, miraculously saved from the sickle, between the yellow stubble of the freshly harvested field, offered itself up red and clean. One could not pick the poppy because it immediately died between one's fingers, like a butterfly. It was best not to touch it. The flowers by the banks of the river were full of evil and perversion. They were beautiful but could not be chewed because they contained fever, a yellow-colored fever that we could envision very clearly. And there was another plant that was not to be touched: the nettle.

It was the nettles by the ruined walls of the meadow that my memory revived, though fleetingly. When the sun heats the nettles they emit a sleepy odor that is unmistakable. I was walking behind my little son, abstracted, drunk with that fragrance, blinded by the light of the August sun, when I heard him cry out, rubbing his leg:

"The nettles stung me!" he said.

I looked at his reddened skin, spiked malignantly with tiny invisible prickles. And suddenly I again heard cries from the past, the wailing of the children we once were, with all those things we knew. I told my child: "If you touch a nettle and hold your breath, it won't sting."

He immediately bent down and rubbed the nettle between his fingers. He kept his mouth shut, slightly trembling, as if there were a bird inside trying to escape. I did the same, intoxicated by his faith, by the sun, by the humming, green fragrance surrounding us, and I felt the sour burning of the nettles on the palms of my hands. But the child turned to me, beaming:

"It's true! Look, it's true!"

I looked at his brown fingers, flawless and smooth, and hid my palms so he would not see them.

We went on looking for mulberries and blackthorn. But I knew, walking behind him, treading on the grass that he had crushed beneath his feet, that what we lose and never find again is not only the names of the flowers that I had forgotten.

MUD

We had so many types of mud that it is difficult for me to remember them all. There was a thick mud, repulsive and black, in certain damp areas by the river, near the poplar trees. Also on the banks of the river there were tiny beaches of sand soft as flour, which when mixed with water formed a powdery mud, almost dry, difficult to scoop up in one's hands, and which had no solidity. It could not be used to mold sand figures. There was also the mud of the flatlands, patiently formed as buckets of water, journey after journey, were carried from the river to the meadows. I know of no child who is not strongly attracted to mud. I remember we used to spend hour after hour in the sun, with our shoulders and the napes of our necks burnt, silently bending over the earth, our hands plunged into the dark and sticky world that drew from within us a pit filled with mystery.

In mud we were one, there were no differences, all of us barefoot and grubby, the rough village boys and the colorless and cautious children of the city. Hour after hour, blackened to the elbows in that bath of earth that dried slowly on our skin, leaving it taut like a scar, we would knead figures, clear and cherished, evocative and full of life. All of us looked alike and seemed friendly, but since those days that seem both so near and so far I have never experienced battles more mute or more secretive than our mud battles. Sitting, lying, squatting, bending over earth and water, we awakened with violent and deceptive force.

Almost always we were silent, and from the corners of our eyes we would peek at the figures the others were making. Brash and nonchalant, we copied one another with no qualms. At times one of us would laugh out loud at a figure that a friend had made. Other times, with no explanation, a hand would be raised and come crashing down on a neighbor's figure. Often the two boys would end up at each other's throats, rolling like two small furies over everyone's mud. And all of us would return home filthy, our noses bleeding. I could not understand why, but that's how it was. I ended up fearing these mud games that still attracted me so much.

There was a boy at our house who was older than us, but short and somewhat deformed, and who ran errands in the village. They said he had had a horrible childhood, full of misery and sickness. Our cook told us that he still could not walk when he was three, and that one day they thought he had died and put him in a coffin, but when his mother cried bitter tears he sat up and stared at her. This boy looked down on our games with a superior, scornful smile. When he passed by, he would hum or spit and look up at the sky. His arms were as muscular as a man's and he never spoke about us, which frightened us a little.

When my father went hunting at dawn, this boy would cross the river and bring him his horse. At times, as if in a dream, I heard the splashing of hooves in the water and on the stones. One morning I was awakened by the sound. I got up and, half asleep, went to the window. A rosy gray light shone on the black poplar trees. I looked down where everything was soaked in dew, and saw the boy. I looked at him and suddenly understood the feeling that dominated us, this feeling that has so often surrounded and imprisoned us throughout our life. Standing still, he looked at the little mounds of dry mud that our figures of the day before had become.

They were small, sad, deformed mounds of meaningless earth. But he must have seen in them other figures, other people, perhaps the yearning for all that was forbidden and hopeless; the figures of his small world, miserable and dull. He approached the figures, and lifting his bare, broad, callous foot angrily crushed them, cursing quietly to himself.

THE BUTTERFLY CEMETERIES

When the flood waters of the river had receded and the old sunken village once again emerged, I remembered our secret burials, the burials that we held as children on the eve of our return to the city. Each of us held a burial, special and private, sad and filled with joy.

We took our precious treasures to a hidden place. Everyone chose a special spot, secret from brothers and friends, so that no one could desecrate it. We brought skull-shaped stones, stones like boats and like blue and red coins. We brought a key, a horseshoe, bits of colored pencil, and once, I remember well, an iridescent scarab, green and gold, in a matchbox. We would look for earth that was soft and friendly, and dig into it with our hands or a small hoe, and bury everything. We would remember the place, the shade, the tree, the stone, or the fountain. "Next year I shall return!" we told our buried realm. The worst tribulation we could suffer was if someone discovered our tombs and desecrated them.

Once this happened to me. The culprit was a boy we called Pinitos. He used to run errands for our house. He must have followed me when I went to the woods carrying my box of treasures and my small hoe. The following year I went to my tomb and found nothing. There had been frost and snow; weeds had grown as always, but the musty objects, rotten and pale with memories that had become speckled with time, did not appear. Nothing was there. There was no point in looking around, thinking I had made a mistake, I who had such good memory for such things.

At night, when the crickets sang and we went home for dinner, Pinitos stood by the meadow fence, smiling strangely.

"Well?" he said gruffly. And that "Well?" made my heart jump.

"What?"

He held out his warty hand and took me to the twin poplar trees. My world collapsed. My treasure, which he had dug up, lay there dead.

"Tough luck!" he said.

With his heel he started stamping on my things as if he wanted to beat them back into the ground, as if he wanted to tell me: "Look what I'm doing with your little bits of trash, that's all they're good for!"

From then on I never buried anything again. That warm night with its high stars marked the end of the glowworm, butterfly, and poppy cemeteries.

Only now, seeing the village of my childhood musty and

hollow, disinterred with its trees of stifled silver in the great August heat, do I feel that same emotion of years ago. The feeling that took us to friendly trees, to the horse-shaped rock, to the snow-cold fountain, in search of a little piece of lost time.

Translated from the Spanish
by Peter Constantine

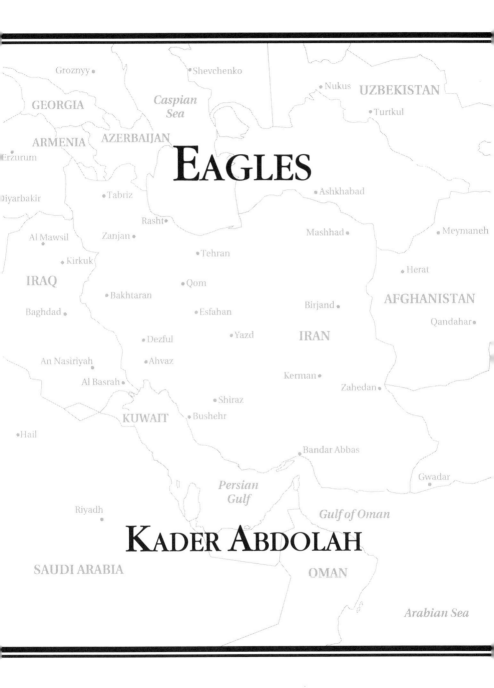

Kader Abdolah was born in 1954 in Iran into a family with a rich literary tradition. His great-grandfather was a poet and is considered the founder of modern Iranian literature.

Mr. Abdolah undertook undergraduate studies in Teheran. In the early 1980s, he illegally published two novels on the Kurdish struggle for an independent state. He fled Iran in 1985 and emigrated to The Netherlands, where he became fluent in Dutch. In 1993, his first book written in Dutch was published in The Netherlands to critical acclaim. Since that time, Mr. Abdolah has given readings and lectures throughout The Netherlands and Belgium. The following selection is a short story from his collection *De adelaars* (The Eagles).

Mr. Abdolah lives in The Netherlands with his family. He is currently at work on a new book.

One stands on the mountains of my country as if on a grave. An abandoned grave; no one knows who lies buried there.

During the winter nothing is visible. In spring when the snow has melted, the graves emerge, but they are quickly covered again with wildflowers. It is as if nature were afraid that the graves might be discovered.

When mountain climbers come across such a grave they start singing songs against the dictatorship. They approach the grave, singing. They set down their rucksacks to rest a bit and to eat.

They leave the remains of their food for the birds, for the eagles that fly high in the mountains. The birds soar over the grave waiting for the climbers to leave. Instantly they dive in a mass onto the food.

The eagles are a sort of guide for the climbers, flying in advance and letting them know where the graves are.

Standing on the highest peak of my birthplace, looking toward the northern mountain chains, you often see flights of eagles plunging down.

With the naked eye you see only the gray-blue mountains, but with binoculars you can also see the villages that lie among the crags. Small villages that, like graves, are covered in winter by snow and in summer by wildflowers.

My father was born in one of those villages, and my brother lies buried in the mountains.

I did not know that my brother had been murdered. I lived in the capital, and he had been in jail in our hometown as an opponent of the regime.

"Come immediately!" my father said on the phone. It was one o'clock in the afternoon. The message was frightening, knowing my father. "Come immediately!" meant as much as a bullet in the head.

I quickly drove to my hometown. At a quarter to five I reached it, but I could not go to my parents' house until it was completely dark.

At three minutes to five I parked my car in the neighborhood and then carefully walked home.

My father had seen me through the window. Before I reached the house he came out.

He greeted me curtly, as always. It was as if he had not telephoned me, as if I had driven 300 miles for nothing. But I knew him. He never showed his emotions.

He just looked at me, and by the glimmer of light from the window I could read in his eyes what I had feared. I knew the story: a corpse, a father, and no grave.

My father had picked up my brother's body, but as it was "unclean" it could not be buried in an official cemetery. We would have to bury him silently, in secret.

My mother stood by the window, staring at me. She wore black. According to our custom she should weep, shriek, bang her head, and tear out her gray hair. I would run to her and hold her hands, and we would then cry in each other's arms.

But that was absolutely forbidden. We could not let our sorrow be seen by anyone. No one must know that my brother had been murdered in prison.

In front of the door stood a dark-red delivery van. I knew at once who was in it, but I did not want to believe it.

"Let's go!" my father said, and he gave me the key.

I held the key of the van in my hand. It was reality, but I had to see my brother with my own eyes in order to believe it.

So I went to the van and opened the rear door. There he lay crumpled under a white sheet. He looked cold, lying on his right side with his hands between his thighs. They had crammed him into the van. There was not enough room to stretch him out full length.

I turned on the overhead light. His head was uncovered.

It was my brother, with a bullet in his left temple.

My mother was still standing by the window. Behind the glass she looked like a black-and-white photograph of a mother who had passed away.

"We have to get a move on!" my father said.

I closed the rear door and got behind the wheel.

"Where are we going?"

"Up there!" my father pointed to the northern mountains.

How could he be so cold-hearted, when his son was lying behind him in the van, dead?

I couldn't figure out what my father intended to do. I knew that he was not the kind of man to allow his son to be buried in a desolate place in the mountains.

I wanted to look him in the eye, but I didn't dare. I wanted to speak with him about our sorrow, but he wasn't that kind of man.

So, silent, I drove to the northern mountain chain.

My father had always been a closed book to me; I couldn't understand him.

In my thoughts I always see him sitting on a Persian rug reading the Holy Book.

He had always read the Book fervently; after my brother's death he read it with even greater zeal.

That's how he was, and I, his oldest child, dared not ask him: "Father, why do you not read any other books?"

He always tried to find his own answers to his problems, and when he couldn't find them he consulted the Holy Book. Now I wondered where he got his faith.

"Do you have a plan? Where are we going?"

"We are going to Marzedjaran," he said.

"To Marzedjaran?" I asked, astonished.

That was impossible. The inhabitants of that village were extremely religious, and they surely supported the dictatorship. We couldn't just ask them for a grave.

He said nothing, but it was obvious to me that he had

consulted the Book. There was no point in discussing the matter, so I drove on.

The road lay deep in snow. It was impossible to see, except for the tracks made by the tires of the village buses. Driving on, I tried to remember the last time I had seen my brother, but I couldn't. It was as if all my memories of him had disappeared with his death. In their place an image appeared in the blaze of our headlights: A group of men were leading him to the firing squad. They had tied a black cloth over his eyes, and his hands were shackled behind his back. He held his head high and shouted something. I couldn't hear his voice, but I could see his mouth move. It looked like an old silent film. He was shot three times. I could tell by the convulsions of his body. Then he got a bullet in his left temple. His head fell forward, like that of a dead bird.

I looked at him in the rear-view mirror. He lay there with cold eyes. What color eyes *did* he have?

Blue? Gray? Blue-gray?

There he lies now with his hands between his thighs, and I can't give him a book anymore.

What was the last book I had given him?

We were almost at the village. I could see the outline of the houses. No lights were burning; it was as if light had not yet been discovered. When we drew near, I saw the smoke from the bathhouse, the only sign of life.

In a village like this, people always wait: Somebody comes, somebody leaves, a child is born, somebody dies. The sleepy village always waits for something to happen; then it comes to life.

We drove into the village. We did not have to announce ourselves; a car in the dark meant certain action.

Who would be roving about the mountains in winter? No one but a resistance fighter, someone on the run, or someone lying dead in the back of a van.

We had just what they needed for a long winter: a body with bullets in it.

Suddenly I heard barking. I quickly turned off the car's lights, but to no avail. The dogs had picked up the scent of death, and they ran toward us through the snow. Then I saw the men—three heavily dressed men with sticks.

"Allah!" my father called out.

The dogs, barking, blocked the way. The men approached us.

"Stay in the van!" my father said, and got out.

He went up to speak to the men, to tell them that he was a friend of the Imam of the village. He stretched out his hand to them, but they rejected it and came toward the van. They looked at me angrily and walked toward the rear door. My father ran to them. The dogs began barking again, hard. I got out too quickly. My father pushed the men to the side and stood with his back to the door. One of them grabbed him by the sleeve and pulled him away. The others opened the door. A dog jumped into the van. I quickly seized a jack that was lying there and hit the dog hard on its back. It yelped loudly and jumped out. Furious, I pushed the men out of the way and stood there, ready to defend the body with the jack in my hand.

The men threw themselves at me and started beating me. My father shouted, "Allah!" and tried to push them off, but they pushed him roughly into the corner.

I heard more people arriving. They wrenched me away from the men and pushed them back. I looked about in fear. The whole village had come out.

They had formed a circle around us and were staring at us silently. Suddenly my father broke the stillness. He reached out to them and cried: " I beg you for a grave . . . I have my son's body in the van."

There was no reaction, no answer. It was as if they were made of stone, petrified people staring at us full of astonishment.

The men approached us again.

"Be gone, sinners! No grave for you!" one of the men shouted.

"I am begging you for . . ."

"Away with you!" the man shouted wildly and ran toward my father.

I raised the jack again, but my father snatched it from my hands and said: "We will go away!"

I returned to the van. Tears burned in my eyes, but I could not cry, since my father was there. I got a grip on myself, but then suddenly broke into sobs.

When we were far enough from the village, I looked at my father. I was shocked. He sat next to me, a broken man. I could tell by the way he was sitting that he had asked the Book for guidance and it hadn't worked. He was like a bird with clipped wings.

I could not bear it.

I drove aimlessly through the mountains, waiting for him to get his strength back. After a long time he drew a deep breath and said: "Allah is testing me."

Deep in thought, he pulled the Holy Book out of his pocket and started looking for guidance.

It was too dark to read, but he didn't need light. He knew the whole book by heart. He read like a blind man; touching the pages, he knew where he was.

It took him some time to figure out. Then he put the Book back in his pocket and said calmly: "We will go to Saroeg."

I disagreed with him. I couldn't see the difference between Saroeg and the village we had just escaped from. We could go to a hundred villages, but the result would always be the same. He wouldn't bury his son secretly. He wanted a formal grave, and that was impossible. He had to accept it. We needed to talk to each other to find a solution, but for him that was inconceivable.

*   *   *

The cemetery of Saroeg lay just over a mile from the village. It was a bare, icy place.

"You can wait here. I'll go to the village myself," my father said.

I stayed alone.

The moon was shining, but to me that was no comfort. I was deep in thought. My father was right! I suddenly realized why he was adamant about finding a formal grave, in spite of the great danger.

I was ashamed that it had taken me so long to understand. We had done nothing wrong. I grabbed the jack, thinking that men and dogs would come again.

This time I would guard my brother at all costs. I wouldn't let anyone approach the body. He had fulfilled his task; now it was my turn. He had to be buried properly. When one day my children ask what we did against the dictatorship, we can show them the grave and tell them about the burial.

I felt like a wounded tiger, a tiger with a bullet in its neck. I was ready, tooth and nail, to tear dozens of men to pieces. I waited for the men. I waited.

I heard people approaching. Five men carrying lanterns. I shook with rage, but they were old men, and my father was walking in their midst. They had no dogs with them. I understood. We could not bury him here. I could see it by the way they walked. They were friends of my father. All they could do for him was walk him to the end of the village. They wanted to show him that they felt for him. They knew the spies of the regime and were aware of what could happen if they let my father return alone. They were as religious as he was. Perhaps they hoped that they might find a solution as they walked him back. They approached me, to greet me, to offer their condolences, but I couldn't face them. I opened the door of the van and got behind the wheel. My father bade them farewell and got in.

*   *   *

We were driving off when we heard someone calling.

"Wait! Stop!" my father shouted.

I stopped the van. He rolled down the window. One of the men came running up, out of breath, and stuck his head in with its long white beard.

"You . . . must . . . go to Rahmanali!" he said. "Rahmanali is the only one who can help you."

My father nodded a couple of times in agreement.

The man then looked at me.

"My condolences, young man! Be calm! You must resign yourself; this is Allah's will."

I looked into his old eyes and silently bowed my head.

"Drive to Djeria!" my father said. "We shall look for Rahmanali." I drove to Djeria, where my father had been born, my grandfather had lived, and my great-grandfather was buried.

For a moment I had to think where I had heard the name Rahmanali. I knew him. He was a small old man with a long gray beard. I met him a few years before in Djeria when I had been looking for my roots. I had wanted to find out more about my great-grandfather who lay buried in the mountains of Djeria. His tomb was a shrine. He was known as a saint, but my father denied that. At home the subject of my great-grandfather was taboo. Through this silence we had gradually forgotten him. But I had wanted to know, and on a warm summer's day I went into the northern mountains to Djeria to find him.

Arriving at the mountain where he was buried, I saw groups of pilgrims with mules climbing to his shrine. I also saw many eagles in the air.

I was astonished. I had not expected this.

I joined the pilgrims in the climb. I was curious to see the grave and expected a traditional shrine—a tomb with burning candles, full of fragrant incense and covered with colorful tapestries. But it was just a simple grave, without even a headstone. A lonely grave at the foot of an enormous gray-blue boulder.

"Why is he buried in such a lonely place?"

No one could say, but people told me what they knew about him.

"He was shot. A bullet in the head."

"Why?"

"He was a resistance fighter on the run. He was alone, and they were many. He escaped into the mountains. They cornered him and shot him dead."

"And what happened then?"

"They left him to be devoured by wild animals, but he was secretly buried."

Everyone told a different story, but in every story there were bullets, escapes, and men stalking.

A wise man told me: "If you want to know the real story, you must go to Rahmanali. He knows everything. He knew him, and it was he who buried him."

I was told that Rahmanali went to the mosque every day at five, and that I would meet him at the village square. I went to a teahouse in the square and sat on a bench by the door to wait for him. At five on the dot, all the men in the teahouse ran outside. I stood up.

"What's going on?"

An ancient man with a long gray beard came up the square toward the mosque. He had a stick and walked straight. He looked as if he came from another time. The men from the teahouse walked up to him, knelt, and kissed his hand.

He was 104 years old and was known as a saint. Word had it that he could perform magic and had brought dead children back to life.

When I saw him, I lost all desire to meet him. I did not want to kneel in front of him. He was venerable, a symbol of old age, of religion, like a figure out of the ancient tales of the village. He was unapproachable. I went back to the bench and finished my tea.

Suddenly halfway to the mosque he stopped, turned round, and came directly toward me. I quickly stood up again. He stretched out his ancient hand toward me and looked me in the eyes. I took his hand respectfully, but I did not kiss it.

Who could have known that three and a half years later I would be kneeling before him to kiss his hand?

Who would have thought that on a wintry night I would run through the streets of the village looking for Rahmanali's help?

My father and I drove to Djeria.

"When one leaves one's birthplace, one never knows how one will return," my father said. "I would never have thought that I would be linked with Djeria again, but now I have to bring my son's body here."

I couldn't understand how Rahmanali could find a grave for us, a formal grave. In Saroeg the old man had told me to resign myself to my fate. What else could I do? I waited for "Allah's will."

As we approached the village, I again turned off the headlights.

"I will go to find him myself," I said.

We didn't want to ruin our last chance. Everyone here knew my father; if he were seen, people would immediately know what was up. My father agreed that I should go. He told me that Rahmanali lived in a small street near the square, opposite the mosque.

I knew where the mosque was, and I also remembered the street.

The best way to get there, I thought, was to go along the river. That way I could reach the square with a minimum of danger and without having to cross the whole village.

"Till later," I said and started off toward the river.

"Wait!" my father called.

He ran toward me.

"If you run into trouble, call out Rahmanali's name. When he hears you, he will appear and you'll be safe."

I had to hurry. We didn't have much time. I started running over the frozen snow. The dogs would not be able to hear me yet.

It was cold and the whole world looked frozen. The river was completely covered with ice. I ran, thinking of my father's words: "When Rahmanali hears you, he will appear and you'll be safe."

I had to find Rahmanali before the men of the regime could grab me.

If they grabbed me, I would shout "Rahmanali" so loud that even if he were in the deepest sleep, he would wake up.

I entered the village cautiously. After four or five streets I arrived at the square. A foreign scent in the middle of the night in winter could only mean trouble. The dogs had smelled me. Behind me, one of them began to bark. The whole village was about to wake up. What was I to do? Run, or walk as if nothing was wrong? A big dog jumped over a wooden fence in the street in front of me.

Now or never, I thought to myself, and started running.

Throughout the village, dogs started barking. The big dog raced after me. I ran harder and saw startled villagers in front of me in the street. A group of men tried to stop me, to grab hold of me. I pushed them away with all my force and shouted out: "Rahmanali!"

Tears filled my eyes. I ran blindly toward the square.

Everyone knew now where I was heading.

Now or never, I thought, and shouted with all my might: "Rahmanali! Help! I'm looking for help for my brother."

Suddenly an old man with a long gray beard appeared. He wore a long white nightshirt. I quickly knelt before him and grabbed his lean hand. He pulled me up without letting me kiss his hand.

"Be calm, my boy! You are safe," he said in his old voice. The dogs barked no more. They hung their heads low and wagged their tails.

The villagers went home.

When someone went to Rahmanali, everyone had to disappear. He was the holy man of the village.

He took me into his house. I told him who I was, but he had already recognized me.

I did not have to explain. He knew exactly what I wanted of him.

All I said was that the van stood outside the village and that my father was waiting for us.

He went to the stable to get his mule.

A little while later we were going through the village streets. All the lights were out. The village had fallen back into its winter sleep.

My father had heard the barking of the dogs. When he saw me with Rahmanali, he hurried toward us, embraced Rahmanali, and for a few seconds held him tight.

"Let us be off!" said Rahmanali. "It will be daybreak soon."

I opened the rear door and heaved my brother onto my shoulder. My father rushed over to help me. We laid him over the mule's back.

I got the shovel and the pickax out of the van and shut the rear door.

"Let us go!" Rahmanali called.

The mule started for the mountains.

My father looked at me in surprise.

Where are we going? I could read in his eyes in the moonlight.

I was about to say something when I heard the sound of wings. I looked up. A large flock of eagles were flying ahead of us.

Translated from the Dutch
by Peter Constantine

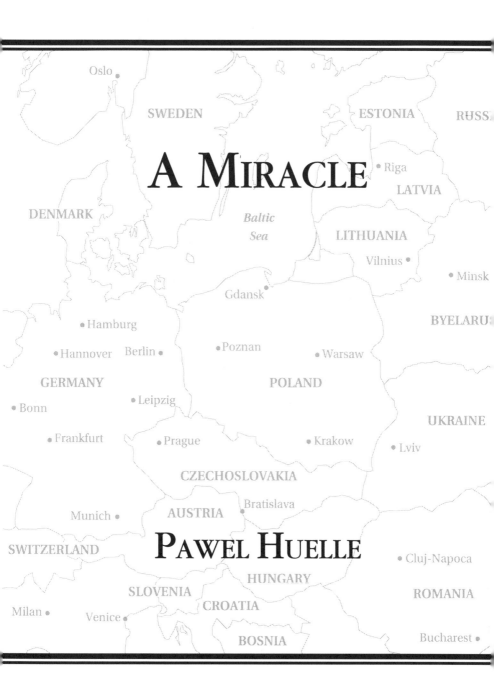

A Miracle

Pawel Huelle

© Andrzej Taranek

P awel Huelle was born in 1957 in Gdansk. Critic, editor, poet, and novelist, he also worked as a journalist for Solidarity. His first novel, *Who Was David Weiser?*, has been translated into several languages and was shortlisted for England's *Independent* Foreign Fiction Award in 1991.

The following selection is excerpted from his forthcoming book *Moving House and Other Stories*, to be published in February 1995 by Harcourt Brace.

 T he local nursery was called Ksawery's. People used to say, "I'm off to Ksawery's to pick up some tea roses," or, "They've got the best tomato seedlings at Ksawery's." In actual fact, however, there was no Ksawery. State Horticultural Center Number 17 was run by Beefy Handzo, who smelled of beer and sweat, had a leucoma in his left eye, and spoke with a dreadful accent, as if he'd just emerged from the mines to the surface of the garden plots in Upper Wrzeszcz. So why did everyone say, "I'm going to Ksawery's"?

No one has ever explained it. Perhaps, long ago, before there were any Prussian hussars' barracks or an Upper Wrzeszcz, someone called Ksawery lived there. I don't know, but I did hear that Handzo had been such a lackey to the Communists after the war that the underground passed a death sentence on him. That was why he fled Silesia and came to seek his fortune here on the coast, where the local Party Committee gave him a job as manager of the nursery.

I was extremely curious about Handzo. Whenever I saw his belly overflowing his flannel shirt or bumped into him among the growing frames as he shouted benevolently to the female workers, I shivered. There was an indefinite yet distinct aura of death hovering over him. If he were to be found one morning riddled with bullets (best in a hot-house full of flowers), my dim daydreams, my secret longing for some real partisans to show up in our city would have come true. Sometimes in my sleep I'd hear a loud squeal of tires and imagine a black Citroën braking on Reymont Street. Then three sullen-looking men in leather jackets and knee boots would walk up the narrow path between the pansy seedlings and along the boxwood alleyways. Finally the morning silence would be shattered by the rattle of machine-gun fire and the crack of a pistol shot, its echo resounding far. Handzo would fall onto the soft earth among the orchids and perennials, and the black Citroën would speed away toward Bretowo, vanishing around a bend in the highway. But the years went by and Handzo went on doing fine. The Communists shot a lot of partisans, and many others were forced to surrender their weapons, but the ones who managed to get out of prison and come back from Siberia didn't feel much like shooting any more.

Anyway, Handzo knew all about gardening and especially about growing flowers. His roses, cyclamens, peonies, irises, and carnations, his cinquefoils, chrysanthemums, and asters, and the orchids he grew in greenhouses, were all the most beautiful in town. Three times a year I would buy roses there, and each time I felt great joy at the thought that I'd soon go through the iron gate and between the long flower beds, that I'd wander among greenhouses from which a tropical scent of damp earth and plant stalks emanated, and I'd see pyramids of flowerpots with the workers in their blue overalls among them. Never have I seen women who were so happy at their work. They used to sing songs or tell jokes followed by loud peals of laughter. They gave off a scent of vegetable tops, soil, cheap tobacco, and flowers, and this unusual combination of smells, which I could sense from a distance as I gazed at their crouching figures, their gingham head scarves and blue blouses flitting about in the sunlight, filled me with rapture. I was sorry my mother wasn't one of them—then I could have come here every day to be close to their warmth, which permeated my body and went spinning around and around inside it. But my mother didn't work at Ksawery's, and the only times I ever came here were before her name day, before my father's name day, and before the arrival of Grandpa Antoni, who came to see us once a year, usually in the last few days of August.

"Go to Ksawery's, "Mama would say, "and buy five roses. Best of all Goldstars. But if the Goldstars have spots on their petals like last year," she pondered slowly, "be sure to ask for the America variety. You won't forget? Goldstars or Americas."

My father was fond of his father-in-law, but he found all these preparations and the atmosphere of a special occasion very irritating.

"Why go rushing off to buy roses?" He asked the same question every year. "Is Antoni a woman? No, Antoni is not a woman," he'd answer himself loudly, "and he's sure to think those flowers are absurd."

But Mama knew what she was doing. Whenever Grandpa Antoni came, it had to be as it was before the war: a white tablecloth and soup served from a porcelain tureen, not poured from a jug as on any other day. After the second course came the obligatory fruit drink, and dessert as well, and on the table in a crystal vase stood a bouquet of roses. Everything had to be just as in the past: For a short while the clock would turn back and there would be no reminder of the view that lay outside the windows of our apartment.

"What a performance!" my father would say. But even he could tell that the crystal vase, the roses, the porcelain tureen, and the silver teaspoons I'd spent the whole afternoon polishing were not really symbols of the past, but a challenge to the present. When I brought the roses from Ksawery's, Mama tenderly held them, stroking the petals against her cheek, and arranged them in the vase one by one. It was a moment of happiness for her: She had everything ready, the living room was bright with sunlight, and we were about to go to the station to pick up Grandpa Antoni.

He'd appear on the platform with his leather suitcase, wearing an unbuttoned trench coat and a hat at a slightly jaunty angle, coming toward us enveloped in a odor of coal fumes and locomotive steam. Amid the shouted greetings of travelers, the crash of doors closing, and the rumble of mail trolleys we'd hear his voice: "So, my darlings, how's life in this godforsaken Hanseatic city?"

That year, however, when everyone was talking about Handzo's illness and saying he wouldn't last much longer, Grandpa Antoni gave us a surprise by sending a telegram that read: "FLYING FROM KRAKOW STOP BE AT AIRPORT MONDAY STOP LOVE ANTONI STOP."

"Why isn't he coming by railway?" my mother wondered. "He always travels by train. What an extraordinary idea!"

"Everyone gets a little eccentric in old age," my father said. "What's wrong with that?"

But she wasn't listening. Hunched over the printed form, she read the message several times, and her expression was worried as well as disbelieving. Even the roses I brought from Ksawery's on Monday morning, with purple petals and droplets of dew on their stems, could do nothing to change it. Mama didn't like new situations, startling changes of plan, and unexpected telegrams. They never brought any good, and to her mind they always foreshadowed trouble. We took the number 2 from Victory Avenue, the 4 from the Philharmonic building along Karl Marx Avenue, and finally the 7 which dragged itself relentlessly up Feliks Dzierzynski Street, and when we reached the tramway loop near Gedania Stadium her face was pale as if the sequence of tram numbers contained some unsettling significance. Soon we were standing outside the airport terminal, looking at the light aircraft and some old biplanes by the hangars. A slight breath of wind stole into the air and ruffled my mother's hair as an announcement came over the loudspeaker that the plane from Kraków was delayed: An instinctive twitch ran across her face, and I felt her touch my arm. But that was only the beginning.

A quarter of an hour later, there was a feeling of nervousness among the crowd of people waiting. The silver silhouette of an Ilyushin had not yet appeared in the clear blue sky, and the loudspeaker was silent.

"Why don't they say something?" fumed a lady in a black toque. "They should give us an explanation!"

"They don't know themselves what's happening," said a man with a dachshund on a leash. "Right, Josif?"

Josif barked merrily and wagged his tail as his owner expounded various hypotheses to the audience. Maybe the compass was broken. Or perhaps the chief pilot and navigator had fainted. Maybe they were forced to crash-land in Torun or Grudziadź because of a leaking fuel tank.

"Please don't go on!" a young man in glasses interrupted. "Let's go to the information desk."

Several people followed the bespectacled fellow to the terminal building. Mama did not budge. She stood with her hands on the metal barrier, its red and white stripes like a border post, and stared into the sky as if the airplane would appear in a moment or two. But the sky was empty. Meanwhile, the delegation came back from the terminal building; the information desk was closed.

"It's a scandal!" said the lady in the black toque. "Treating us like this!"

"Worse things used to happen in the war," stated the man with the dachshund. "When I was dropping bombs on Hamburg, they got us right in the guts, my dear lady— we had to jump into the English Channel. Right, Josif?" The dog turned its head excitedly, but this time it didn't bark or twitch its tail. "Luckily we were fished out by a British submarine. I've sometimes thought they ought to have parachutes in passenger planes, because if a fire broke out, for instance . . . or if both engines suddenly cut out . . . what would happen then?"

"They don't have parachutes?" said the lady in the black toque, suddenly terrified. "Is that really possible?"

Mama glanced up at the people who were talking. Her

green eyes, which sometimes went brown, had taken on a shade of gray, as if ashes or autumn clouds were reflected in them.

"They've only got life jackets, in case of a splashdown," said the dog's owner. "But you can't have a splashdown over Warsaw or Bydgoszcz, can you?" The dachshund started yapping excitedly, the lady set her black toque straight on her head, and the young man took off his glasses and wiped them on his handkerchief. At that moment, somewhere on the torrid air of that August afternoon that rippled across the baking concrete, dry grass, and arched hangars, we heard the distant but unmistakable sound of engines.

"There!" the young man cried. "It's coming from over there!"

Indeed, a moment later the silhouette of an airplane came into view. The Ilyushin's silver wings and fuselage gleamed in the sunlight like armor, and the low hum of the engines grew louder and louder.

The plane flew over some red-roofed houses and its shadow was already gliding down the runway when suddenly, just when it looked as if it was ready to land, the engines began to sound at a higher pitch, the pilot stepped on the gas and raised the rudder, and the Ilyushin, with Grandpa Antoni on board, went shooting past the airfield, gaining altitude until it topped the clump of trees in the cemetery at Zaspa and vanished over the sea.

The crowd went into an uproar. Several people ran back to the terminal building, while those who stayed at the barrier spoke in fragments.

"The rudder . . ."

"The steering . . ."

"The brakes . . ."

"A wing . . ."

"If it was the steering or a wing," said Josif's owner, "it would have been lying in pieces hours ago."

The lady in the black toque began to cry. Someone else began to whisper a prayer, but it was a stage whisper; every word of the "Hail Mary" was clearly audible in the baking air, after which a churchlike silence reigned.

Suddenly the sound of engines could be heard again. The Ilyushin was on its way back from the bay. It reduced altitude rapidly and its fuselage rocked several times, but then it gave up again on landing and flew across the airfield as if tied to an invisible thread.

"The pilot must be drunk!" the young man shrieked. "A second more and he wouldn't have lifted the plane. What an imbecile."

"No, no," retorted the dachshund man. "It's just that he can't release the undercarriage. It's obvious, my friends."

"Oh my dear God!" cried the lady in the toque, wiping her eyes. "What do you mean, he can't release the undercarriage?"

"He can't lower the landing gear, madam. It's called a wheel blockage."

"So what's going to happen?"

"We'll see. At worst a belly landing. Without wheels."

"Without wheels? Oh, my God!"

"It can happen. I once landed in Halifax, in a Lancaster that was heavy as a tank, and we had a similar problem."

"So what happened?"

Every one fixed their eyes on Josif's owner.

"It was all right," he replied calmly, with satisfaction even. "The navigator broke three ribs, and the gunner cracked his head, right here on the forehead."

"Were you all right?"

"I had a few bruises. And then I got three weeks' leave in Scotland. Right, Josif?"

Josif barked merrily, and everyone burst out laughing. But the laughter didn't last longer than two wags of the dog's tail.

The R.A.F. veteran went on to explain that the pilot of

the Ilyushin would have to keep flying until the fuel was used up ("There's nothing worse than hitting the runway with the belly of an aircraft when you've still got some fuel in your tank"), and as he was describing how the airplane would have to land "on its very last drops" without losing speed and without crashing into the ground at the final moment, Mama said, "Let's get away from here. I have to call your father."

The terminal building was rife with confusion. Pilots' white caps, dark blue uniforms, and gold buttons were flashing in the rays of the sun, stewardesses were nervously running from corner to corner, their heels clicking, and military men grouped by the bar were drinking soda water, wiping sweat from their faces, and talking loudly. Like a monotonous refrain, the words "smash," "crash," and "hit" were frequently repeated, as well as "crush" and "slam."

Mama had no coins, so she went to the cash desk to change some money. As she stood there, and then as she dialed my father's number at the pay phone, I inspected her blue and white flowered dress, her white handbag, and the new sandals she'd put on for the first time that day. The slender straps embraced her ankles delicately, then ran from silver buckles down to her toes. I knew that all this had been chosen with Grandpa Antoni in mind; she always wanted to please him, she never told him her troubles, and she loved him very much.

The call went through and she shouted into the receiver, telling my father to leave work at once, take a taxi, and hurry to the airport at Wrzeszcz, repeating the same thing several times in an exasperated tone, because evidently my father couldn't understand whether the plane had already crashed or was about to crash. As she passed the receiver from one hand to the other and tossed her head to flick back the hair that was falling across her forehead, I kept thinking about Grandpa Antoni and about parachutes, which—as the R.A.F. veteran had said—the silver

Ilyushin didn't have on board. If only it did! If Grandpa
Antoni had a parachute, he'd be sure to order the door
opened and then boldly leap out and glide like a bird above
the city. I could see him flying toward us, getting bigger and
bigger above our house on St. Hubert's Street; I could imagine the parachute canopy hanging in the branches of the
chestnut trees. Grandpa Antoni would cut the straps with a
pocket knife and jump to the ground. Or what if he landed
at Ksawery's, in the middle of the nursery, somewhere
between the rose field and the growing frames? He would
instantly be surrounded by the women, each one offering
him flowers, and though Handzo would start shouting that
something was fishy, that he must be a spy dropped during
the day by mistake, the women would laugh loudly and
escort my grandfather to the iron gate. He'd come knocking
at our door with a large bouquet of roses, the America variety, and say, "I've never had such a welcome!" Though he
had never been a paratrooper, he had been a soldier, and
when he was pursuing a tsarist and later the Bolshevik
army, marching through villages and towns to kick
Budyonny out of Poland, he was always surrounded by
women who strewed flowers around him. In return, he'd
salute them, not because one of them was his wife or his
fiancée, but because he was the sweetheart of all the women
as he went off to die for each and every one of them on the
field at Radzymin, Lwów, or Warsaw.

Mama replaced the receiver, and we went back out into
the blazing August afternoon. The plane had come back
and was now skimming over the roofs of Wrzeszcz.

"It's a Soviet make," said the young man in glasses.
"Once it gets jammed, that's it!" Before he had time to go
on, the Ilyushin descended lower, and at some point above
the railway tracks the left undercarriage hatch came open;
with it came a wheel.

Everyone began to shout like mad, but their joy was
short-lived. The right hatch was still stuck, and the left one

and its wheel refused to fold away again in spite of evident attempts by the pilot.

The roar of the engines grew louder and louder. It looked as if the plane was coming in to land again, and amid cries of "What's he doing?" "He'll kill them! He'll kill them!" I heard my mother say, "No! Oh, God, no!"

Then the pilot did something that defied the laws of physics: He brought the plane down almost onto the runway and struck the protruding wheel against the concrete surface. Then with a macabre growl from the engines he raised the Ilyushin back up into the air and flew off steadily toward the sea.

"My nerves can't stand it," said the lady in the black toque. "I just can't watch."

The snapped-off piece of undercarriage shot down the runway, the steel arm spitting sparks like an anvil, until finally the broad wheel broke off from its shaft and bounced onto the grass, then hit a hangar wall, which took the impact with a hollow thud.

The dachshund yelped wildly. Wailing ambulances were driving up from the direction of the city, and my mother, head raised, was following the silhouette of the airplane. Now that it had gained enough altitude, it was circling the airfield like a lazy beetle.

"But he had to do that!" Josif's owner was shouting. "He had to! Do you people realize what landing on one wheel would mean?"

The lady in the black toque grew faint, and the first ambulance crew got busy. Some medical attendants laid her on a stretcher, slammed the doors, and, siren blaring, rushed her off. Meanwhile more ambulances kept arriving, as well as gleaming red fire engines that drove onto the runway and drew up in battle formation down the side of the hangar. Firemen began unreeling long canvas hoses, sunlight glinting on their helmets; from a distance the stretchers laid out on the grass looked like deck chairs at a health resort waiting for some happy patients.

Spectators from the city were arriving at the barrier, including some newspaper reporters with cameras. I kept thinking about Grandpa Antoni, and about death. Is he very much afraid of it, sitting up there watching all these preparations through the window? Is he praying for a miracle like the other passengers? Which was better: a sudden death from a bullet or an accident, or a slow death that visits a sick man's bed day by day and takes a little more life away with it? It keeps coming back to take more, toying with the man, tormenting him, until they close his eyelids and light the final candle for him. Which was better: dying in an airplane, unable to say goodbye to any of your nearest and dearest, or having to say goodbye to everyone in a hospital?

The plane went on spiraling above the city and the airfield. For several weeks now Handzo had been dying in his bed, crying out at night, "from pain and fear," rumor had it, "between shots of morphine." The moment of death was still far ahead of him, out of view. He didn't know when it would come upon him, and he must have been feeling that in spite of everything he'd go on living. That feeling wouldn't leave him until the very last, whereas up there in the sky Grandpa Antoni, free of any pain or illness, was being led to his execution.

What could he be thinking of? Me? Mama? Plane travel? Of the fact that we're all doomed, and the only honorable way out is to make our own choice of the time and place of our death? Or maybe he was thinking about the roses cut for him this morning at Ksawery's, or the ones that had once saved his life.

When he had returned to his city after the war and found a fiancée, he bought her a small bunch of roses with the last of his money and said, "Marry me—but first I'll build a house." Soon after that he met Rozenfeld, and they set up shop together, running a consignment warehouse and dabbling in the timber trade. Everybody warned him,

"You'll fall flat on your face, Antoni!" but Grandpa just smiled, and every week he took his fiancée a bouquet with one more rose in it. Business was good and the house was almost finished. When the new furniture had been moved in, Grandpa Antoni took his fiancée a bouquet of sixty-seven roses and officially asked his future parents-in-law for their daughter's hand. Then they all sat down to tea, Viennese pastries and wine. Never once did he suspect, as he and his fiancée danced the waltz, the mazurka, and the polka, that his fate, fortune, and prosperity would soon crumble more easily than the Viennese pastries. That very afternoon the great New York crash began; a few days later the shock waves hit the stock exchanges in London, Paris, and Berlin, flowing onward ever faster, passing through Warsaw, until at last they reached his town. A week before his wedding Grandpa Antoni had nothing left but five suitcases stuffed with paper money. And it didn't stop there—the bank notes kept multiplying at a giddy rate. Soon there weren't enough suitcases to hold them, or even enough trunks, until at last the warehouse office was crammed with them from floor to ceiling. Rozenfeld and his family fled abroad, probably to Budapest, and on his wedding day Grandpa Antoni was left with no consignment warehouse, no house, and no new furniture. All he had was a dozen drawers filled with Polish marks—his own and Rozenfeld's. He could buy flowers with them, but not bills of exchange. So he took the money to a gardener, asked him to make up a fine bouquet of roses in exchange for the lot of it, and after hurriedly jotting down a farewell note, he sent them by courier to his fiancée. Then he went for one last time to the house that had never been their home. He touched the furniture fondly, stroking the banisters, upholstery, and walls. As he was putting the gun barrel to his temple, sliding his forefinger across the cold trigger, he suddenly heard a voice. "Antoni, for the fear of God! Is your life worth less than paper money?" It was his fiancée.

"How did you find me?" he asked, putting down the revolver. Then Grandma Irena—who wasn't a grandmother yet, or even a mother—fell into his arms and said in sobs that if he had sent the letter on its own, without the bouquet, she wouldn't have known where to look for him, but those roses, those beautiful Goldstars and Americas that he'd bought for several quadrillion Polish marks, had sent her straight here and told her to run on wings if she wanted to be in time for a wedding, not a funeral. And although they never had their own home or warehouse again— from then on Grandpa Antoni sold Elektrid radios made in Wilno—every year on the anniversary of that day, in remembrance of his wedding and his rescue, he bought his wife a bouquet of roses, nothing but Goldstars and Americas.

Anyway, Grandpa Antoni might not be thinking of any of these things up there—perhaps he believed a miracle would save him again.

My father came forcing his way through the crowd, which had become denser. He was in quite a state; he'd had a hard time finding us. His face was grim, his brow furrowed, and his linen shirt was stained with sweat under his arms. He hugged my mother and held her close against him, and she burst into loud weeping.

"It won't work!" she kept saying. The plane would crash. She wouldn't even be able to speak to her father. "We never took the boat to Hel together! There are so many things we never did," she said more softly.

My father stroked her head and gave no answer; in a situation like that it's better not to say anything. The plane went on circling overhead. When it went climbing laboriously upward it looked like a silver cross, and when it dropped or tipped sideways as it changed direction it became a shining question mark.

No, Grandpa Antoni wasn't thinking about death. More likely he was wondering what he'd have for dinner, or where he'd go for a walk the next day. Maybe to the pier at

Sopot? Or perhaps to the Opera Forest? Or maybe to the old entrenchments and redoubts where we went every year to fly kites above the moats? From up there he could see it all perfectly, and I envied him that view. Imagine seeing the entire city and the bay as it appeared on the map! Imagine being able to see the ports, shipyards, churches, streets, hills, and the narrow strip of beach all at once, a view you could never get normally, not even from the top of St. Mary's tower. It struck me that Grandpa Antoni was a poet, a kind of artist, who had boarded the airplane with the sole aim of experiencing some extraordinary impressions of landing and then describing them in his memoirs. He didn't actually write anything except letters, but then he didn't really have to: I was his living memoir. On our walks in Green Valley or on Bukowa Hill he taught me far more than the names of birds and trees— he entrusted me with the past, which now lived only inside him, a past that probably no one knew as well as I did. The images of Grandpa Antoni's life were recorded in my memory, as on the pages of a heavy volume; it was enough to evoke a single one of them to set the rest in motion.

I could see the face of the German who had stopped Grandma Irena, hit her on the head, took her bicycle and the food she'd gone to get in the countryside, and said, "You're a Jew! You've run away from the ghetto!" I could see my grandmother's face, standing there on that cart-track in the early afternoon, as the German military policeman unslung his gun and said, laughing, "Now I'm going to kill you!" Then I could see my grandfather's face, as she was telling him about it, safe and sound back at home. I could even hear her voice, repeating over and over, "What if he had shot me? What if he had shot me?"

Overhead the plane completed another lap, and the flash of sunlight on its wing brought another flash to mind, the light bouncing off the river when Grandpa Antoni went fishing so that Grandma Irena wouldn't have to go to the country any more and so no more Germans would grab her along the way. Grandpa stares intently at his float, squinting. He senses that nothing will come of it today, no fish soup or fried barbel, maybe just a couple of perch. His eyes are worried and sad, but not just because of the fish. Beyond the forest, long bursts of machine-gun fire rumble in the distance, and on the sandbank among the willows the hollow rattle echoes loudly, carried by the water. Grandpa Antoni knows what those bursts mean, and he can't understand what has happened to the world—it has lost its center of gravity, it's reeling and stumbling about like Jacob by the ford of Jabbok. On his way back to the city, his creel empty, Grandpa sometimes enters a deserted church, falls to his knees, and tries to pray, but no words of prayer will come into his head. He looks up at the image of God, despondent on the cross, and goes back home to Grandma Irena and my mother even sadder, and not just because his creel is empty.

As the plane was turning another gleaming circle, my instincts told me nothing bad would happen, for up there in that tin machine, sitting at his window, my grandfather was having the very same thoughts I was. And if we were both having the same thoughts—he up there in the sky and I down here on the ground—if both of us were turning to the very same page in the volume of his life and taking a careful look at it, we were bound to see one another again. Not up there, in the blue and empty void, but down here on the earth.

Once again I saw Grandpa Antoni by the river. There he was on the bank at dusk, pulling up his line, but the hooks were empty, so he cast it back again, the lit a small fire in the shade of a willow tree and sat warming his hands over it. He pulled the line out of the water a few more times and cast it back again, because he hadn't caught a thing. A cool breeze wafted from the river, and just as he was thinking it was too bad for fish soup and too bad for times when owning an Elekrid radio, or any radio, was forbidden, as the twilight of July 1942 was falling over the marshy meadows, Grandpa Antoni saw the man. He was about thirty years old; he wore ragged gray clothing and looked as though he'd been hiding in the willows for a long time, or had come out of the forest. "You don't have anything to eat, do you?" the man asked. "No," replied my grandfather. Then it occurred to him that the man must be terribly hungry and might not have eaten for ten days or more. He reached into his bag and took out a stale roll, the day before yesterday's, which he'd kept for bait. Feeling ashamed, he said, "This is all I've got. Take it and eat it." The man smiled; shaking his head, he said quietly, "Cast it on the right." Not until later did Grandpa Antoni realize that when the stranger said "on the right," he meant on the right side of the rock that protruded from the surface of the water. It was strange advice, but Grandpa took it. He baited the line and went back to his fire. The stranger reminded him of the handsome cantor Josele, the rabbi's son from Monasterzyska, though he didn't really resemble either the father or the son. Maybe he was just a ghost? No, he couldn't be. He was sitting now by the blazing embers and gazing at the water. His manner, like the advice he'd given, was strange and puzzling, but Grandpa didn't ask any questions, so they sat there in silence for some time. Then the man stood up and said, "Thank you," and when Grandpa asked what he was thanking him for and why he was off so soon, he answered curtly, "I must go," and vanished among the willows as quietly as he'd appeared. For a while Grandpa thought it was a dream, but it wasn't, for when he pulled up his line it almost snapped under the weight of fish.

The plane turned yet another circle, sunlight glinting off the metal fuselage as if off the scales of a fish. Mama was weeping in my father's embrace while he comforted her as best he could. The young man in glasses and the owner of the dog called Josif had disappeared in the crowd. Finally an announcement came over the loudspeaker that the landing would take place shortly. Everyone was requested to please remain silent. The medical attendants and firemen jumped into their red and white vehicles and turned on their motors, ready to drive onto the runway. Then I remembered something else: My mother couldn't stand fish. Almost every day until the end of the war she'd eaten the zander, pike, roach, and eels that Grandpa Antoni used to bring home by the bucketful.

The Ilyushin was coming down to land. I stood on tiptoe at the barrier, holding my breath. Mama didn't want to look. My father held her head against his breast as if she were a little girl. The plane dropped lower and lower, until we heard a dry crack, then something like a hollow whistle, then another crack as if a gigantic sheet of canvas had been ripped apart. At last there was a mighty clang of metal and a grating sound that went on for a very long time. Coming slightly off the concrete runway, the plane plowed into the grass. The fuselage was leaning on the left wing, which had broken. Smoke was pouring from underneath.

The fire engines went first, and after them the ambulances. Then we waited—only about two or three minutes, but it seemed immeasurably longer—until the firemen had doused the entire fuselage in dense clouds of white foam, and from that great white snowdrift the passengers began to emerge through the rear doors of the plane. Among them we spotted Grandpa Antoni. In his unbuttoned trench coat and with his hat set crooked on his head as always, he came walking diagonally across the grass, taking no notice of all the commotion and the firemen's shouts. When he was halfway across, he noticed us and hurried over to the barrier.

"I'm seventy-three years old," he said, "and I'm very sorry that at my age I cause you trouble."

"That was a miracle," sobbed Mama, "that was a real miracle."

Two weeks later, as we were seeing Grandpa Antoni off at the railway station and he was regretting that he wouldn't be taking an Ilyushin 18 back from Gdansk to Kraków, I remembered one more thing I still had to ask him. In that spot by the river, had he ever caught fish on the right side of the rock before? Before he met the Jew from the woods, I meant.

"Maybe not," he answered. "No, I don't remember."

"What Jew from the woods?" asked Mama, evidently alarmed, but the train had just pulled in. Grandpa Antoni got into the sleeping car and my father handed him his suitcase through the window. The conductor's whistle, a hiss of steam, and the roar of the engine drowned out Grandpa's final words as he said something more to me through the opening.

"What Jew were you talking about?" Mama asked again. "What's the story?"

"Oh, let him be," sighed my father. "Why can't they have their little secrets?"

Several days after Grandpa Antoni's departure, Handzo died in the hospital, "after great suffering," people said. He had refused the priest and didn't want final sacraments, but his wife spoke to the parson, and on the quiet the parson sent a curate who, after the Party funeral, furtively said a prayer and sprinkled holy water on the cross she had had put up.

A month later I went to Ksawery's to fetch roses for my mother's name day, but they didn't have any Goldstars or Americas left. I bought some tea roses, and as I was walking between the greenhouses, past the growing frames and rows of boxwood, it occurred to me that the black Citroën would never turn up on Reymont Street now, and I would never ask Handzo if a sentence of death really had been hanging over him.

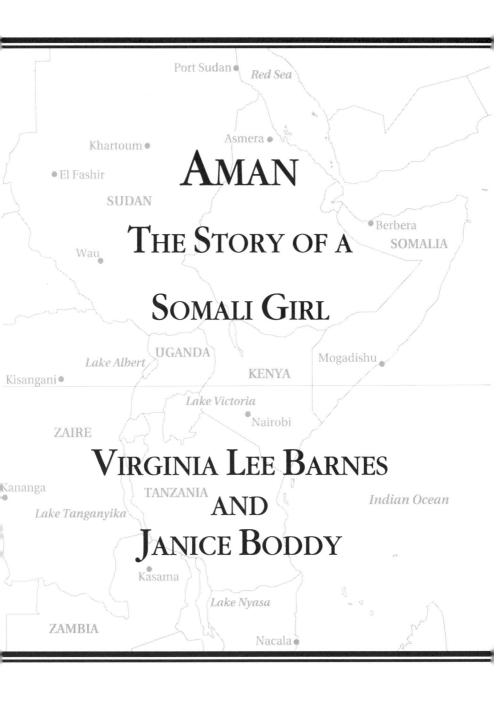

AMAN

THE STORY OF A

SOMALI GIRL

VIRGINIA LEE BARNES
AND
JANICE BODDY

© Erin Elder

Aman was born in Somalia. The daughter of a chief, she was nonetheless limited by economic hardship following her parents' divorce. She was defiant and soon left home in search of opportunites beyond those of her village. "Aman" is a pseudonym used to protect her family from any harmful repercussions that might arise from having her story made public.

Virginia Lee Barnes was born in 1942. She worked in Africa with the Peace Corps for two years, did research among the Lugbara of Uganda, and worked in refugee camps in Ethiopia and Somalia. She taught at several American universities. In the late 1980s, Dr. Barnes met Aman and prepared a written account of her youth based on extensive interviews. Dr. Barnes died in 1990.

Janice Boddy completed the preparation of Aman's story for publication. An associate professor of social and cultural anthropology at the University of Toronto, Professor Boddy has conducted research among the Muslim women of North Africa since 1976. She is the author of *Wombs and Alien Spirits* and countless articles.

The following selection is excerpted from *Aman: The Story of A Somali Girl*, which will be published in September by Pantheon Books.

Mama's business was going downhill: When Grandmama died, Mama had to spend a lot of money for the funeral. We had seven days of reading the Koran, and people came to eat and to give sympathy to Mama—seven days, day and night, twenty-four hours. We had food ready all the time for all the people; some of them came from a long way away in the country. After that, Mama was short of money and couldn't afford to go on a long trip to get butter and the other things she sold in the market. When you're really poor and you're angry, you see things the wrong way. Mama was down when Grandmama died, like me. That's why I went back to work, so the money could go to Mama—the 150 shillings I made I brought home, plus all the tips I got. Now I was growing, and I began to buy all my own clothes. Before, Mama bought them for me. (Daddy used to buy clothes for me for special holidays too, when he was around, after my parents divorced and my father remarried.) I began to buy things I liked: shoes, a scarf, a belt. But I was sad because of Mama's situation. All I could think of was how to make more money—that was my one idea. The more I grew, the more the problems grew, and I got tired thinking about how to make money to help Mama and everyone else I loved, and myself.

By this time I was grown. I was born in 1952 and now it was 1965. I was thirteen. I remember I was thirteen years and seven months old when I was married.

A relative of mine, a cousin of my mother's—I called him uncle—his wife had just had a baby, so he called me one Friday to help her. He took me in his Land Rover to the market to buy the food. He gave me money and told me what they needed, and he waited for me in the Land Rover while I went to buy the things, and when I was finished we went to their house. That's when I first met him—my future husband. He was a friend of my uncle's from Mogadishu. My uncle had a maid who was a big woman, but she had Fridays off. So I cooked for them and washed the dishes, because when women have a new baby they don't cook unless they have to. They have to rest and stay in the house for forty days and play with the baby.

After this man saw me at their house helping out two or three times, he started to talk to me. I knew something was going on, but I didn't know what it was. They talked about me, and looked at me when I took things to the table and when I brought them something and when I dumped the ashtrays. He looked at me in a different way.

He began to come over to their house almost every Friday, and it went on for about two months like that. My uncle told me, "This man is my best friend." He told me the man's brother was a government minister. He told me they were a high-level family. He told me the man liked me and the main reason he came to the house was me. I said, "Oh, that's why you all talk about me and look at me so funny." And he said, "Yes, you're a clever girl, you understand. Think about what I've said." And then he used words I hated; he said, "Think about your mother. All of you need help, and this man can help." I hated that. I really did. The first thing in my life was my mama, because of all she had been through and all she had done for me, and I didn't need someone else reminding me, but that's what he did. I felt hurt. I got angry and told him, "I'll think about it," and I left.

I walked and walked for miles and miles, just thinking about what he had said and what I felt, and tears were running down my clothes. I was talking out loud to myself—repeating what he had said and thinking why he had said that—because of money? I walked until I couldn't walk any more. I sat down and got angry and cried again, and I prayed to Allah to help us. I sat and I thought and thought and thought. And I decided to go for it—to get married to him. I didn't have money. I didn't have my boyfriend Antony, who had been sent to Europe to go to school. I would get married, at least to get money and be somebody. I thought: Maybe you can even see him—your boyfriend—one day. Because you'll have money, you can go back to school and finish your education—because Antony was from an educated family. I thought maybe I could get away from Mango Village.

In Somalia, in those days, if you don't marry you're nothing. You have to marry, and young, too. Otherwise you'll disgrace your family! It's a disgrace if you don't marry at fourteen, fifteen, sixteen. By the time a girl's eighteen she's too old and it's considered that nobody wants her. At twenty you are superold. I couldn't wait, myself, to get married. My sister Hawa was already married when she was my age. I felt like nobody would want me. They were saying I was bad, so I thought I might never get a chance. I wanted to show them I could make it. And I knew that once I married, I could divorce and they wouldn't say I was a girl, they'd say I was a woman, a *divorced* woman. I'd have a little freedom. I could do what I wanted.

So I decided to marry this man.

I went home. I was dirty, and I had tears all over my face, and my feet were filthy, because I had been running and walking fast. I took a shower. I was tired, and I fell asleep. The next day, after work, I stopped at my uncle's house and told him I had been thinking about what he had said and I agreed to marry his friend if he would accept what I wanted. My uncle said, "What do you want?" I told him I didn't want him to tell my father's side or anybody; we would just go get married, he and I, and after we came back we could tell my father. But before the marriage, I didn't want him to ask my father or wait for my father to give me away or ask my brothers. Because usually your family negotiates. The man has to come and ask your family, and if your family says no, and you really love him, you run away together and get married. From where you live, it has to be a hundred miles away. The Muslim religion doesn't allow you to marry close to your family if they don't approve. But if the men in the family say yes, they negotiate how the husband will make your life, how he'll pay and what he'll give the family. They're not selling their daughters; it's about respect. "I raised this beautiful daughter"—and they expect something in return. And it's not buying either. When your daughter gets married and she leaves, there's an empty, empty space. A gift makes you not so sad about that. Also, a father values his daughter, and he needs to know the man won't divorce her or mistreat her. The more money the husband pays, the more the father knows he loves his daughter. And he knows the husband won't want to divorce her if he's given a lot for her. If he hasn't—easy come, easy go. So a large gift lets the father know she'll have some security. That's how our culture is.

But I didn't want to do it that way—unh-unh—because that way my father's family would get the money instead of me. I wanted to get the money from him first, without letting my family know. I told him if he agreed to that, fine, but I didn't want anybody to know until afterward.

My uncle said, "Why are you being that way? Most of the girls like people to ask their father so they don't get a bad name. The way you want it, it's as though you ran away with him, as though you were nothing." He was right. The girls I knew all waited until somebody came along and asked their family for them and paid a lot of money and camels and guns and horses and gold and clothes. He said, "You should be proud. You've got a man with a name and money, and he's ready to do whatever you want—pay whatever you want—because he likes you, and you don't want to do that. Why?" But I didn't want to tell him; even though he was from my mother's lineage, I still didn't want to tell him what my plan was. So I said, "I feel shy, because he's old and from another lineage." He said, "I understand," and he said he was going to tell his friend that I had said yes, and that the marriage would be in a week or two. I also told my uncle to let him know I wanted money—a lot of money. I said I wanted gold and clothes, and I wanted cash in advance. He said, "Don't worry about it!"

I went to my friend Zaytuun's house. I didn't tell her, because I didn't want her to give me good advice, like a sister, even though I knew I was doing things wrong. I wanted to get money so I could help my mama. But even if Zaytuun had known that, she would have told me to stop, or she would have told my mama to stop me, and I didn't want her to do that. My mouth wanted to tell her, but I kept it to myself. She knew I was keeping something from her and kept on asking me, with a nice face, smiling; she tried to make me happy so I would tell her. When I didn't, she got angry and said she wasn't going to speak to me anymore. But I still wouldn't tell her.

That man came on Friday again, and my uncle invited me over to help them. But this time I wanted to watch him, to see how he looked. I told them, "I'll just come. I don't feel well today. I don't want to do anything. I'll just come and keep your wife company." I didn't want to work and have him watch me. I wanted to watch him and see what he looked like, because I hadn't looked at his face that much. Because when you're a girl, you don't look big people straight in the face that much. You look down. I had never looked at him completely. This time, I wanted to see him. I wanted to make sure of what I was getting into.

I felt shy, and my heart was pumping, and I was thinking, "What am I going to say to him if he starts to talk to me?" I had never talked to a big man. I had never dated a big man. I had dated big boys, but I had never dated an old man. That's what he was—an old man.

When I got to my uncle's house, I went into his wife's room, but I left the door open so I could see him. But the only time I could see him was when I went out to the bathroom or the kitchen. Every time I went by, I stole a glance at him. Sometimes he would catch me looking at him, sometimes not. The first eye contact is kind of a little shame. He was a clean old man, nice skin, a lot of soft hair . . . a very nice man. But he was like my grandfather! He was an old man. He was fat, short, light-skinned, with a wide face. He was fifty-five—something like that—fifty-six . . . close to sixty, with a big stomach, a clean body, and clean clothes. You could tell he was from a good family.

The men ate, and I ate a little bit with my uncle's wife. Of course she knew about everything, because her husband had told her his friend wanted me. After we had all eaten separately, the men called me to have tea with them—with just the two of them in the living room. She told me, "Go see them. Don't be shy. Be clever. Be smart." She was young and cute too, and she was married to this man I called "Uncle," who was older than her, but he had a good job, which brought her good money, and she said, "Did you think I married *him* for love? I married him for money. Go!"

I went out into the living room and sat and drank tea with them. The man asked me a lot of questions about my family, especially about my father. I answered all his questions—I guess he was checking whether or not I was stupid, and he could tell I wasn't. He started liking me . . . the way I talked.

That day, after we finished drinking tea and talking, he gave me two hundred shillings. That was a lot of money in those days; it was more than I earned in a month. Our family was living on five shillings a day. So I took it. All I wanted, anyway, was money. From that day on he brought me things every week—clothes and a watch and gold chains and rings and soaps. He used to bring me everything. I really liked it. The more he gave me, the more I liked him; it was like that. Now I couldn't wait to get married.

After three weeks we decided to get married. He spent a night in Mango Village with my uncle so he could pick me up in the morning. I stopped by the night before to make the arrangements. I told him I wanted to leave town early so people wouldn't see me riding with him. He said, "All right." I went straight to see my niece, who was like a sister to me. I told her I would need her the next morning. It took me about two hours to explain to her what was going on, but finally she understood and she agreed to go with me. I went home and had dinner with Mama. I had a nice talk with her and made her happy and told her a couple of funny stories to make her laugh, and cooked tea for her. We had a great, great dinner, and then I asked her if I could spend the night over at my niece's because it was Ramadan and there would be feasting and reading of the Koran over there. She said, "All right." I took the dress I wanted to wear with me and went back to my niece's house.

In the morning we woke up at six-thirty. I had told my mama that I was going to work from there that day and I would see her the following evening when I came home. But I wasn't really going to work, you know, I was going to get married.

We left town in the morning—him, me, and his driver, and my niece. We went to another town—because, as I said, when you run away and you're young you have to go a hundred miles from the town you live in if your daddy or your brother doesn't give you in marriage. We were going to another district quite far away.

You can marry at any age if your father approves; but if

you're on your own, you have to be over fifteen. I was so young; I was tall and skinny, and you could tell I was young, even though I was smart-talking. My husband said he was going to pick up one of his friends to be a witness in case the magistrate suspected I was too young. This man could say he knew me, he was my uncle, and I was sixteen, eighteen, twenty—whatever. So we picked him up, and he went with us. When we came before the magistrate, I lied—I told him I was seventeen. The magistrate looked at me. The other man told him yes—I was seventeen.

That was how we got married. Afterward, my husband paid the magistrate, and we took his friend back to his house and my husband gave him some money. My husband wanted us to spend the night at his house, but I told him, "No, I want to go home." I was afraid that if I spent the night at his house something might happen, and I didn't want that. I didn't want him to touch me at all. So I told him, "No . . . unh-unh, take me home." He said, "What if we stop at my niece's house so they can meet you? I told them about you." "All right," I agreed, "but not to your house." We went to his niece's house, and they offered us tea and cakes and soft drinks, and everybody was saying, "Oh, she's young and cute. She's pretty," and asking me what my name was. I was shy and embarrassed. When we said our goodbyes, they all said they would see me soon.

In the car, about halfway back, I told him he had to give me some money. I wanted to go to Mogadishu; half my family was there—my father's side and my mother's side, cousins, aunts and uncles. I said I needed to go there to buy myself some gold and some clothes. He said, "Sure, don't worry. I'll give you some." He asked me how much I wanted, and I told him I wanted two hundred shillings. He said, "Sure, no problem." I was happy, I was very happy. I said, "All right!" He had a little suitcase, and he opened it right there. He gave me two hundred shillings and said, "If you need some more, let me know." I had never had money so easily. I couldn't believe my heart inside me.

He took me to my father's house, because I was scared to go to my mother because of what I had done. I thought Daddy wouldn't be there. But when he took me to my father's house, he *was* there. He had just come in from the bush that evening. I wasn't usually that scared of my father, but now I had made a big mistake.

Before we went to my father's house we had stopped at my uncle's house—the uncle at whose house I had met my husband—and my uncle had come with us to talk to all the men on my father's side. But my father wasn't doing his duties as chief that night. He was at home. So what we did was, when we got inside my father's house, we separated—my niece and I went to one of the round houses, and the men went to another.

You know, as soon as I got back to Mango Village and saw my father's family, I realized the mistake I had made. I changed my mind. I decided I wanted to be divorced and give him back his money, because I was scared. They took a long, long time to discuss it—almost three hours. We sent the little boys to listen to what they were talking about, and the boys would come back and tell us. Every time they came back they would say my daddy didn't want it. He was saying to my husband, "An old man like you—how did you get married to my daughter? Who gave you permission to run away with my daughter? Aren't you ashamed?" My uncle on my mother's side was trying to calm him down. But my father was saying, "Go get your chief! I want to talk to your chief, not to a half-person, a half-man like you." He was really angry. They couldn't finish the matter that night, so my husband had to leave. Daddy called me and my half-brother, and they started yelling at me: "Why did you do this?" I was really scared, and I told him I wanted a divorce. "Give me a divorce. You're saying I'm too young to be married to him anyway, so I'm not married to him. I want a divorce."

They yelled at my niece too: "Why didn't you tell anybody? You know she's thirteen—you should have stopped her!" My half-brother took me to my mama's house and told her what had happened. She couldn't believe it either—she yelled, and asked my half-brother, "Where did she meet this old man?" He said it wasn't his family's fault. It was her side. I told her he was right—it was her cousin who had introduced us.

The next morning my niece told me my husband had come, with his chief and two or three other old men from different lineages, to talk to my father. They came over to our house around one in the afternoon and said that an agreement had been reached and that they had performed the ceremony again, with my father there, to make the marriage valid. They explained to my mother what had happened, and she had to accept it—there was nothing she could do, but she was so angry!

And I was angry too, because things weren't going the way I had asked Daddy to do them. I had asked him to get me a divorce. I had told him, "I don't want him. I made a mistake. I won't do it again . . ." But it didn't help. My father said, "You chose him," and he had married me to him. He told me that since nobody knew I had run away with this man, we should only tell people about the second wedding, because otherwise it would be too embarrassing for the family. So that's what I did—and though I put the whole blame on my father, it really was my fault.

I went to talk to Zaytuun, to tell her how I had changed my mind and how I didn't want to be married now, and how it had all happened. She asked me why I had done it. Why had I taken his money? I told her, "Well, I knew Mama would stop it if she knew, but I needed the money for myself and for her. Don't you see how down my mother is? Don't you see that she doesn't go out and do her business any more? She doesn't have any money. But now I want out." She said, "Aman, it's too late. Your father agreed, and your whole family has accepted it. Now if you do stupid things"—because I said I was going to run away with the money— "if you do that your family will have to pay all the money back, and then you'll get cursed by your mother and father and by all the people. Don't do that. Wait until you go to your husband's house, and then do what you want. But until you go to his house, don't run away. Your mother will have a terrible shock because she won't know where you have gone, and your father the same, and everybody else who loves you. Stay, and go to the big city with him, and then tell him you don't want him."

I had thought it was easy to be married, but it wasn't . . . marriage was something else altogether. I decided to go with this man I was married to, and get as much money as I could so I could go to Europe and see Antony. I thought it was that easy; that was my dream.

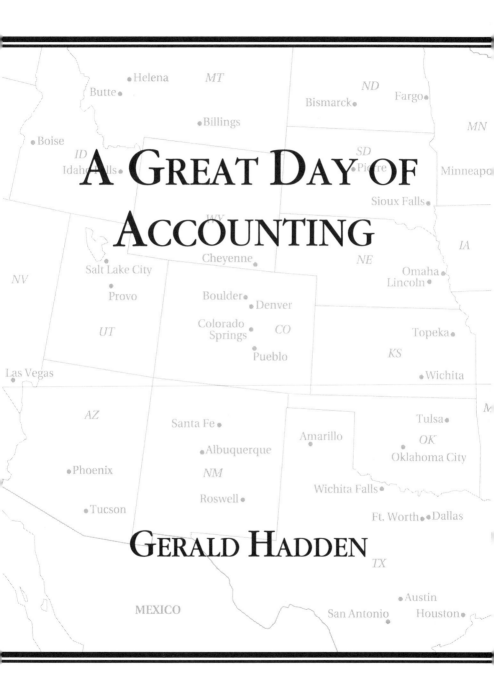

A Great Day of Accounting

Gerald Hadden

Gerald Hadden was born in New York City in 1967. He graduated from Colby College in 1989 with a degree in German, and he spent the following year traveling in Egypt, Asia, and Southeast Asia. Upon his return, Mr. Hadden settled in New York, where he worked at Houghton Mifflin and later International Creative Management. In 1993 he moved West. That year, Mr. Hadden received an award for his submission to *Story* magazine's Short Short Story Competition. More recently, his nonfiction work has been published in the weekly *The Stranger*.

Mr. Hadden currently lives in Seattle. The following selection is his first published piece of fiction.

Delila Tucker sat on the edge of the couch playing with the hem of her summer dress. A slanted shaft of June sun fell through the window behind her, spilling across her delicate back. She glanced anxiously at the clock above the television set. Ted would be home any minute, and then they would be off to somewhere wonderful for three days and nights. Where they were going Delila had no idea. That was the good part. Every year was a surprise.

Today was their tenth wedding anniversary. The yearly trip, destination concealed, had been Ted's idea. Though at first apprehensive about the secrecy, and what it might imply, over the years Delila had come to look forward to these vacations with a maddening and desperate sense of hope. Somehow the discordant coupling of Ted's familiar presence with the utterly unfamiliar setting—musky bedroom, scented bed—made her heart swell with the notion of second chances.

Her hands were perspiring lightly, and she held them palms-up to the open windows. The breeze caressed and cooled them, and as she watched the maples swaying under their new-green canopies she felt that everything was at its most perfect, that it could not possibly have been more so. Then, despite herself, her thoughts turned again to her mother, dead nearly a year ago to the day. The warm weather was bringing her to mind often, and in unexpected ways. Since the funeral Delila had become aware of a peculiar absence within herself—at times so powerful that she might have said it possessed a sort of negative form in its own right. It was as if, now that both of her parents were gone, some last hidden line of defense between her and a great emptiness had disappeared. It impelled her in a nervous and harried way to think about her future, and her children's, and where her faith lay. But she didn't want to start in on all that again. It was a lovely spring day, and outside the cicadas couldn't announce the advent of the season loudly enough. They shed their skins from the effort. Their sprinkler-song rose to a pleasing shiver, lessened, came swirling back like a wind across the sky. The doorbell rang.

Delila leapt to her feet. Ted was a good husband. He had a solid job, something to do with the new computers. She should feel lucky; she was practically certain he didn't play around. Sure, he could be a real boy at times, especially around his old college friends; but like a boy he held fast to his virgin loyalties, of which she felt she was one. She wanted more than anything to love him for this, and at times she was consumed with the desire to reward, to believe. She rushed for the door, past the dining room table where her gift for Ted lay wrapped in gold paper (it had cost a lot, but on her allowance she could afford it), her sun dress and her red hair flickering out behind her, and as she ran she was barefoot. It occurred to her that she might be dressed inappropriately for the occasion; what if Ted were spiriting her off to the mountains? She considered stripping the dress off, right now, for him. That could be her own, small surprise. She swung open the door.

"Delila, what on earth?"

Delila laughed, embarrassed. "Oh, it's you! I was expecting Ted. I'd have been in a lot of trouble if I'd come to the door naked! Give me your bag. Come in!" It was only Ms. Kimball, their elderly next-door neighbor.

"I don't know how you two do it," Ms. Kimball said, shoulders stooped, stepping inside.

"What's that?"

"This sex thing."

"I was just joking. I never . . ."

"Sure, you never. And these are dancer's legs." Charlotte Kimball had a good sense of humor. She kissed Delila, then shuffled to the kitchen and ran herself a glass of water. She knew the house well, having sat for Delila and Ted's two children through each of the anniversary trips over the last nine years, not to mention countless Saturday evenings in between. She'd never married or had kids of her own. Delila thought how lucky they were, having such a kind and lonely old woman as a neighbor. She knew Ms. Kimball relished the time spent with their kids, Sage, their distant and wire-taut whip of a seven-year-old, and Sarah, nine and mysteriously friendless.

Delila thought she understood Ms. Kimball's fervent nurturing instincts, how her lack of children inspired in her such vigilance and care with other people's. Delila trusted her completely. "There's money in the envelope for groceries," she said, following her into the kitchen. "And Ted will give you the address and phone number where we'll be. I should hope! Ms. Kimball looked away. "Or has he already? Ms. Kimball?" Then, with a smile breaking across her face, "You know where we're going, don't you!"

"I don't know a thing about it."

"Now Ms. Kimball . . ."

The doorbell rang again. Delila rushed out.

"Please keep your clothes on, Delila. I'm not a young woman anymore."

"If I inherit the throne it'll be birthday suits for all! My first decree!" What a sharp and funny old bird! Delila thought. Great for the kids. She ran to the door and threw it wide. The sun hit her full force.

"I think your son cut himself."

Reed Van Slyck stood on the front stoop. Reed was the sixteen-year-old from three houses down. Delila hadn't seen him around in ages. He held a stringy arm around Sage's small shoulders. Sage's left hand was cradled against his stomach. His arm from the elbow down was wrapped in a green lawn bag. His stomach and shorts were wet with blood.

Delila felt her legs weakening. "My God," she gasped.

"Let go of him!" She grabbed Sage by the shoulder. Glancing again at Reed, she felt herself rocketing into a fury. She could tell he was stoned. She knew what to look for. His eyes were puddled and cracked red. For a split second she was seized with an urge to bash in his head with a patio stone. But she'd been a nurse, had served for a year in Korea not so long ago—where she'd met Ted. She hadn't practiced since then, but she still remembered the cool-under-fire attitude she had learned. And so she let the rising feeling pass through her.

"Let go of my boy," she managed calmly. Sage watched her with large, shocked eyes. Leaving Reed at the door, she led her son quickly—more quickly than he wanted to go—into the kitchen. Ms. Kimball caught herself on the edge of the sink. Delila grabbed a fresh kitchen towel. She removed the lawn bag from Sage's hand, and it fell to the floor with a sickening thwuck. She looked at Sage's hand and, more strongly than ever in the years since she and Ted had adopted the baby boy, she felt the sodden, unbearable weight of responsibility engulfing her. It pressed on her from all sides, pressed against her very being. Her own voice came to her from far away.

"Sage, can you hear me? Who did this to you?" She wiped his hand, cleaning it as best she could, then wrapped it tightly in the towel. Sage's lower lip trembled, and he shivered. His eyes were wide; she could sense the hurricane swirling behind them. "Sage, I want you to tell me who did this!" The boy stood silent and tense. Inside the towel half his thumb was missing. The only clue to its disappearance was a jagged point of bone and puckered, meated skin clinging loosely around it. What have I done? Delila thought. Sage watched her securing the towel, then rolled his eyes to Ms. Kimball leaning against the counter. She held a bottle of rubbing alcohol in one hand and a bar of soap in the other. She held them at shoulder height as if about to perform a magic trick. The boy's knees gave way.

"Ms. Kimball, bring the car around. The keys are on the counter."

"I'll be out front," Ms. Kimball said, snapping to.

"Sage, you're okay. Mommy's seen much worse than this. Do you feel okay?"

"Mom. My fingernail fell off."

"I know, honey. We're going to take you to the doctor." She carried her son to the front door. The Van Slyck boy was standing in the front hall now, shoulders hunched, staring dopily at the portrait of Ted's grandfather hanging above the oak bureau. Reed had run away from home last October, to San Francisco. It looked as if he hadn't had his hair cut since. He was emaciated.

"You get the hell out of my house!" Delila snarled. Reed nearly put his head through the painting, then recovered and slunk out and along the side of the house. "I didn't do anything," he mumbled.

On the sidewalk at the edge of the sloping lawn, Sage's friends sat on their bicycles, feet high on the pedals, wide-eyed, herded together and ready to bolt if necessary. "What have you done to my son!" Delila spat. She stormed down the walk, shaking her fist at the boys. She sounded ridiculous, even to herself, but she was full under a spell now and she was no longer concerned with bringing it under control. Now was the time to get to the hospital. As she neared the curb, the boys wheeled away to the end of the street, then skidded to a stop and looked back. They huddled together like a delegation from a defeated and frightened army.

Ms. Kimball turned the corner, her gray face barely visible above the steering wheel. She honked once, and Delila bellowed hoarsely, "Get the hell out of my street!" The boys pulled their bikes up on the curb, looking thoroughly distraught.

Delila put Sage in the back seat, then ran around the car. "I'll drive."

"I'll drive," said Ms. Kimball.

"Charlotte, move over!"

"Delila, you'll kill us all. Get in."

Delila climbed into the back seat next to her son, but as she was pulling the door shut one of the boys rode unsteadily up to the car. "Hold it, Charlotte," she said.

The boy balanced his bike uneasily with one hand, holding his other arm out straight. He was ghostly white, but as he placed Sage's tattered thumb in the palm of Delila's hand it occurred to her how relative these things could be. For lack of a better place, she laid the digit in the apron of her dress. The boy rode silently back down the street.

Ms. Kimball and Delila and Sage passed Ted coming home from work. He was doing thirty-five. Ms. Kimball was nudging fifty. Delila saw him and, reaching over the seat, pressed on the horn. She held it down, but Ted did not stop. Out the back window she saw him brake, then pull into a U-turn. Then they turned a corner, and she lost sight of him. Please hurry, Ted, she thought. She looked down at Sage lying across the seat, peeking under the towel at his hand. He was filthy. There was blood dried in his strawberry bangs, and his bony knees rubbed back and forth against each other like teeth grinding, belying his incomprehension. His shoulders began to hitch, but when he looked up and caught his mother's eye, he suddenly stopped himself.

"Mom, my fingernail fell off," he said dully and from a great distance, which to a degree was true, and so typical of him.

Two weeks later Delila was thinking hard about going back to school. It was about time, she reasoned. Her kids were both old enough now to take care of themselves for an hour or so after school. Or maybe Ms. Kimball could keep an eye on them. During the day she could go part time and get her nurse's license renewed.

"Well, what do you think?"

"I don't see why you suddenly have to work," Ted said, a little angrily. Since the accident, communication between them had grown somewhat tense. He slipped a marker in his book and closed it. "Look, we're fine. Hell, if business keeps up the way it's going, *I'll* be able to retire in five years." He turned off the lamp on his side of the bed. "We're really doing okay. Don't worry."

But she was riding the new feeling again, the rushed, stricken sensation.

"Did I tell you I ran into Ellen Van Slyck at the supermarket the other day?"

"Hmm."

"What a family, that one."

"How so?"

"You know Reed. He hasn't spoken to anyone in their house since he came back home. Apparently he only communicates by scribbling notes on a pad he's tied around his neck."

"Carl should throw him out onto the street," Ted said from his pillow. "See how far his pad'll get him then."

"He's only home for a couple of weeks to sell his things. Then he's going to hitchhike back to the coast."

"Preposterous," Ted said sleepily.

Delila stared at the broad back of her husband, the rising and falling of his ribs. Sometimes—no, almost always—his view of things was so shortsighted. He'd reached a conclusion before she'd even gotten to her point. She sighed.

"But the really odd thing is, Ellen told me she's saving his notes in a scrapbook. She said she's been working on this scrapbook for years, as a memento for when Reed's older and they're gone. Doesn't that seem odd? I mean, just to include everything, good or bad. A scrapbook should be happy, shouldn't it?" Ted remained silent. This was the sort of thing he never worried about. "Poor

Ellen," Delila said softly, and as she spoke she could not help but suppose that one of the great risks in bringing a child into the world was that one day that child might forsake you.

And yet, she thought, it must be worth it.

Delila watched Ted slip away into sleep. She padded out into the hall. In the bathroom she looked at her face in the mirror. She looked tired, she thought, thin, a little sad. She hadn't slept well since their anniversary, the entire night spent at the hospital. Once again, she ran over in her mind the events of that day—not just as she knew them, but coupled with what she and the other parents had been able to glean from Sage and the boys.

It had started with "The Muppet Show." Apparently there'd been a Scandinavian cook who chopped vegetables and chased Muppet chickens pell-mell about his kitchen with a cleaver. The kids thought this looked like great fun, so the next day Sage and the Kearney twins and David Leonard had taken the Leonards' old mechanical mower out of their shed. They'd gathered a pile of dogwood petals, then raced the mower across the grass until the blades whined and whirred. They took turns feeding petals into the machine, mimicking the Muppet chef's deft chopping, his singsong accent, working themselves into fits of giggles. Sage hadn't paid close enough attention to what he was doing, or maybe he'd been bumped. This was where accounts conflicted, where memories fuzzed over. Whatever the case, when Sage lost his balance his hand slipped within the radius of the blades. The top half of his thumb sailed twenty feet into the Leonards' azalea bushes. Sean Kearney found it. He'd had the presence of mind to bring it to Delila in the car, but in the end it hadn't mattered. The doctors had not been able to sew it back on. The blades on the mower were too dull, they said; it would be more accurate to say his thumb had been swatted off than cut. And Reed Van Slyck, she thought now that she'd been a little harsh with him. If he hadn't witnessed the whole thing from his smoke-filled bedroom across the street, who knows how long the boys would have stood around watching Sage bleed?

Delila turned out the bathroom light. There was a continual and rising sickness in her stomach. She took a deep breath, then shuffled down the hall into Sarah's room. Her daughter was shy, but it had never seemed like a problem. She knew Sarah would grow out of it. She was a highly intelligent girl, and eventually she would learn that and it would be a source of strength to her. It was evident in her handling of her brother's accident: all questions, no tears. Nevertheless, it gnawed now unfairly at Delila's gut. Get out there and make friends if you don't have any, she thought. It's not my fault. The old anxiety, years at bay, blossomed in the darkness around her: So she and Ted had never been able to have kids of their own. They were trying to do the next best thing; that should have been enough. But in the dark of Sarah's room the incredible vulnerability of her children overwhelmed her, draining her resolve. Neither of them was safe, no matter what sort of a parent you were. Still, she'd given them a good life. She had. She wondered where Sarah's real mother was at this moment, whether she'd been as shy as Sarah, or if that was something Sarah had learned from her. And then she thought of Sage asleep on his back, his bandaged left hand lying heavily at his side.

Standing outside his open door, Delila could not bring herself to go in. Not tonight. It occurred to her again, as it had countless times since the morning seven years ago when Sage had been brought to them, that there might come a great day of accounting: when out of nowhere a woman would appear and demand certain explanations. It knotted Delila's heart.

This woman, she would be beautiful and responsible. She would without hesitation assume credit for the child's successes and point an easy finger at Delila for his failures. She would assign penalties for abuse, record for later study Delila's slippery justifications of negligence. *Out playing with a lawnmower?* she might say. *What parent would let that happen? You know what this means. Just think of the things he will never be able to do. Begin to count them.*

Delila sank down until she was kneeling, her head bent low and her long red hair spilling across the carpet. What could she do? Long ago, deep in her heart, she had drawn a correlation between fertility and self-worth, barrenness and despair. What right then did she have raising someone else's children? It seemed absurd that she'd ever believed she could handle it. And so now at last it was coming, she could feel it, retribution closing in like the shadow of a hawk across the field of her mind. Let it come, she thought. I'm finished.

She remained in the hall for a long time—how long she would later not recall. Her thoughts wandered without direction: She wondered about how much nursing school would cost, and about the very futility of that gesture; about the quick years of her life since she'd returned from Korea as Mrs. Theodore Tucker; about Ted's suspected infidelities and what she'd chosen not to acknowledge; about never getting pregnant. In the stillness of her house she began to cry. She thought she would never move from this complicated place. And then, in a moment that she would revisit many times over the rest of her life, she looked up to see her son standing in the doorway before her, blinking and half-asleep, his healing hand held gingerly against his stomach. "Mom?" the boy said, "I'm thirsty." It was enough to sit her up backward against the wall. From there she gained her feet.

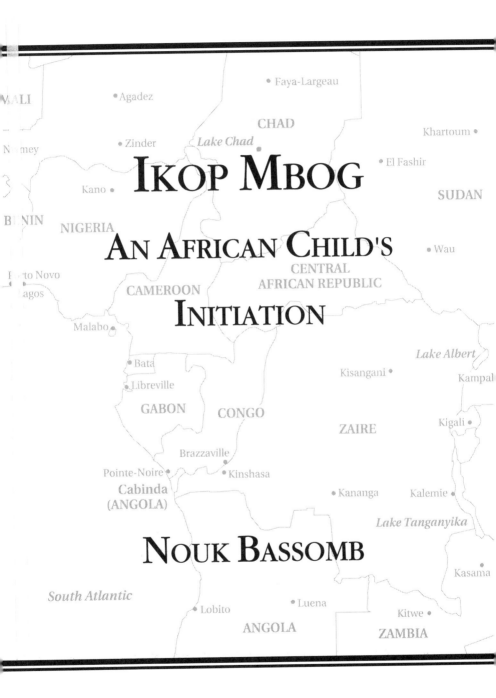

Ikop Mbog

An African Child's

Initiation

Nouk Bassomb

Nouk Bassomb was born in Cameroon, Africa. At age twenty, he was arrested for distributing leaflets in support of a workers' strike and was held in a concentration camp for four years without trial. He subsequently studied in France, where he received a Ph.D. in archeology from the Sorbonne. After moving to the United States, he started doing field work in New York City homeless shelters and was so moved by what he found there that he set up the Homeless Self-Help Program to assist homeless men.

Dr. Bassomb is the author of a memoir relating his experience in the concentration camp in Cameroon and two volumes of plays on the political situation in his native land, all of which were published in France. He is a storyteller and writes on various subjects, including myth, tradition, and rites of passage. He is currently working on an account of the three-month initiation he underwent in the African rain forest in order to enter adult society. The following selection is excerpted from that work.

Dr. Bassomb lives in New York City.

My responsibility as a Bassa initiate is to "keep the flame alive in my father's house." "Keep the flame alive in your father's house" are the words I heard over and over again during the three months I spent in the bush learning how to make myself ready to enter adult society. And at the end of this difficult period, the elders said: "Go now, and even if there seems to be no one in the entire compound, keep the flame burning in your father's house." They said it as though I had never heard this injunction before. So this is my duty, my task, my responsibility. When one is assigned such a job, one discovers that the best way to keep a flame alive is to give it away. Everywhere I go, whether in big cities or small villages, people are always asking me for fire, generally to light a cigarette. I always carry fire with me—a lighter or matches—even though I am not a smoker. I know that when the moment comes and I myself need fire, someone will say, "Here's a light."

Even if there seems to be no one in the compound, keep the flame alive in your father's house . . . But who is my father? Is it my biological father, Bassomb, son of Batama? Is it all the men in my village who are my father's age or all the men on the planet who are my father's age? Is it my culture, Bassa people's culture, which we call Mbog Bassa? African culture? Or human culture, everything human? Or all of the above? Who is my father? Is it purely and simply Hilolombi the Creator? Who is my father? "We give you a container," Samnik Mapuna, one of the elders, replied when I was thirteen and asked him these questions. "You fill it up. Whatever you put in it is what will be in there for you. Just go ahead and do the task assigned to you. Fan. Blow. Add dry wood. Remove the ashes. And stay awake."

"But you insisted that the beginning and end of society is in the 'We', not the 'I'," I argued when he repeated that each man has to discover for himself what it means to keep the flame alive. "You know what to do, and you do it," he said, but I didn't know what to think. That's when he looked at me as though I were a ghost and, somehow losing his temper, said, "Keep talking, boy. In the meantime, babies are coughing. Don't you hear the babies coughing? Women will wake up tomorrow morning with sore throats and elders with pneumonia in their chests. If the people disappear, for whom would you keep the flame alive? We are just praying for the life of the people." He held my hand very paternally, took me aside, and said: "If you want others to accomplish this work for you, why don't you put a goat to roast on the fire? You'll see what will happen. Children will come running. They are always the first to come. Then the passersby will stop to rest and have a good meal. Women will also come looking for their children and wondering why the children are drawn to the fire. 'What's going on here?' they will ask and when they see what's happening, they will take control of the situation. They always do. They will call their daughters and ask them to bring the condiments, all the secret spices and ingredients they keep for great events. Before you know it, the passersby will have water to wash with and quench their thirst. The elders will come also, with kola nuts, palm wine, and lots of stories to tell. Go where you want to go. That fire will stay alive as long as the goat cooks."

If I raised the question of modern technology and progress with Samnik Mapuna, he would look at me with that expression I know so well, asking, "Didn't I do a good job with you, O Nouk, son of Bassomb, son of Batama? Didn't you learn anything? Did I waste my time? You worry about the winds of change. Is there wind? Fire has no better friend. Wind? How could wind destroy the fire?

That happens only when the fire is covered, overprotected. Expose the fire. The wind will fan and blow it for you. Just add wood. And remove the ashes. Open it up. Today the whole world is father's compound, the Mbog your father's house. Tomorrow, the universe will be father's compound, and our planet father's house. Move with the times. Call everyone to the celebration. Welcome everyone to the feast, and when the passersby have their strength back, give them a little of the fire to take home. If it's good enough for them, it will become part of their household, and before you know it your fire will be burning in' millions of households. People will come from all over the world, saying, 'I've heard that your fire is best; that's why I've come from China or Portugal, Sweden or Australia.' Don't be fooled. They don't come for the fire, but for the entertainment surrounding it. Everyone likes stories with happy endings, but also each person wants to feel as though he or she belongs to something strong, a group where he is noticed, cherished, where everyone knows his name, where women will offer him a cup of water because they know he is thirsty before he actually says so."

When I was thirteen years old Samnik Mapuna, the elder responsible for initiation that culminates in circumcision, led me and twenty-five boys of my own age into the bush for three months. During this time he taught us many things—to hunt, to work, to dance, to think, to heal, to understand and embody the creation myth, and to inherit our place in the tradition of our tribe, for it was his task to bring us to the point where we were ready to enter adult society. What follows is the account of several days during this unforgettable period of my education, known as Ikop Mbog.

*   *   *

After a day in the bush we ran back to the camp. The fire was burning and the smell of the goats roasting was hanging in the air. The tom-toms beat continuously, as if they were summoning ghosts to the event. Dancers from the surrounding villages were flexing their muscles. The scene was exciting to me, and everyone was preparing for the search for Gwek's grave. "Gwek, son of Kooy, son of Ndombi," the Nkuk singer began with a quiver in his voice, "the founder of this clan, had seven male children. All founded lineages, but today only those of Hiko, Ngon, Sagal, and Makuk have survived. This is proof that the flame is dim and the fire is dying, when there's nobody in father's house to revitalize it." Everyone repeated the words, singing them with the same intonation. And the tom-toms supported the sound with their staccato beat.

"Once Nkuk starts," the saying goes, "it will last all night long." Nkuk is a rhythm. Nkuk is a dance. Nkuk is a ritual. Nkuk is continuous percussion performed by four to eight musicians who beat the tom-toms and thwack flattened pieces of metal cut from oil drums. The rhythm shifts from clicking and clanging to the sound of footsteps stomping on the ground. This music is invigorating and exhilarating, and the dancing men gradually enter a trance. From time to time the dancers drink a brew that stimulates them on many levels, and eventually the place is transformed into a battlefield. "Once Nkuk starts, it will go all night long." That night it was pretty well advanced within two hours. The rawness of the music, the brew, the musicians, the personalities of the dancers, were a potent mix. Before I realized what I was doing, I found myself shaking on the dance floor. Someone had to reach out and pull me back because I was in the way of the master dancers who needed the whole forty feet of clearing to express themselves.

To dance Nkuk is not a difficult thing. Two groups of four to five dancers approach from both sides of the floor, meet in the middle, and continue to the other side. Sometimes they return, sometimes another group takes over. This makes Nkuk a sound and motion relay. The warlike way the dancers move—close to the ground and jumping like frogs—gives the scene a surrealist dimension. Nkuk is also an interactive game. There is a lead singer, and the audience repeats his song. His center-stage routines, coaxing the audience into joyous foot-stomping, come as interludes between multipercussion revels and bursts of energy.

This ceremony had been organized to take us to another level of understanding. We had to find the grave of our ancestor. What did that mean? How would getting drunk, hallucinating, and entering into a trance help us in this quest? Was Gwek's grave a physical reality or a mental state? At that moment, I wasn't thinking about any of these things. I cared more about eating goat meat, drinking brew, dancing Nkuk. From time to time, I struck the biggest drum in the clearing and played the most extraordinary percussion instrument in the show—two small aluminum cans that had to be banged together to keep the rhythm even. Everyone found something to beat, time to dance, to eat the goat meat, and to drink the brew, and the night became a Nkuk adventure.

Nkuk was beyond anything I had ever experienced. What gave it its unique quality was not only the energy from the brew, but also what took place in our minds. Our ancestors had taken their ideas and discoveries from I don't know where and fashioned them into a rite that stretched the boundaries of reality beyond the firmament. There is something in the human mind, something that holds the key to life itself. We had to discover this while we were still young. "Once you become an adult," Samnik told us later, "it's too late."

When the cock crowed, we left the camp at a run.

*   *   *

It was nine days since we had left the camp. And none of us had had much sleep. We walked, stopping only for a two-hour rest, and then walked again. I didn't know where we were going. I walked along the path next to Samnik, and I had a sense of closeness I had never felt before. He held my hand firmly, warmly, very paternally, as though he didn't want me to disappear. Up to this point, he had preserved a no-nonsense attitude that left no room for play, especially when it came to our initiation. The clan had entrusted this man with the task of making us ready to enter adult society. Not only did N'nenes ("the initiator") have to do it, he had to do it well. From day one, he made it clear that there would be no questioning his instructions. And he kept his distance, coming to us only to teach, direct, or give an order. But these last nine days had been different. He had never stopped joking and laughing with us. Why did I have the premonition that today was not only different but special? Were we in a life-and-death situation? I tried to pull my hand away but the man held it tight. I felt as though I had to extend myself beyond anything I had been through in the previous twenty days. I was tired, sleepy, hungry, and thirsty. And I couldn't even complain. That would have put a stigma on my entire lineage. Where were we going? I didn't know, but each time we reached a crossroads, he told us firmly: "You can still go back now, no question will be asked of you. But let me tell you this, we'll soon reach a point of no return." What could a thirteen-year-old boy do by himself in an unfamiliar area of the rain forest? How about the prospect of shaming his entire clan? N'nenes would call someone's name, and the boy would answer: "Let's continue!" That's what he was supposed to reply. We had already passed eight crossroads, one each day. N'nenes stopped at the ninth: "If you pass this line," he said, "it'll be for good. There's no turning back. What do you say, Massing, son of Massing?"

"Let's go!" the boy replied.

He asked us to run. We ran. And here we were in front of a cave. It looked as though no one had ever been in or out of it, for cobwebs obstructed the entrance. We could easily have broken through the webs and entered the cave, but instead he made us remove the strands one by one. "Make sure you don't destroy them," he said gently.

For some reason, I remembered the hunters we had met a couple of days earlier. They were trimming a hunting net. Samnik insisted that we learn the rudiments of this craft. That night, he had allowed us nine hours of sleep on the beach, but we had our feet in the water, which was especially uncomfortable. Now, his facial expression was the same as the one he had worn that day. "If trimming a hunting net can help us later in life to get our food," I found myself thinking, "how could a cobweb help us?" In a few minutes, because there were a number of us working on the project, we had removed the webs from the cave's entrance. Our initiator instructed us to observe them closely and keep in mind how they were made. Then he asked us to put them back over the entrance to the cave, this time from the inside. "They might help hide someone chased by warriors from who knows where." That's when I understood what we had been doing. It hit me like lightning. We had reenacted the myth of our origin by repeating the acts of Nanga, son of Nanga, the founder of our ethnic group. So we were at the rock called Ngock-Lituba. "I've been told, Pap," I said to him, "that this rock can be seen from afar, but I don't recall seeing it."

"You did," he answered. "If I'd warned you yesterday that we'd reach Ngock-Lituba today, you would have seen it. We have eyes, but sometimes we just don't see."

We cleaned the cave and ate the cassava cakes, dried meat, and fruit we had brought with us. Before I knew it I was dozing off, but I was awakened a few moments later by my neighbor. When I opened my eyes, Samnik was talking: "During the time you are here, we'll have a period of study every morning, every afternoon, and every evening. By the time I finish with you, you'll know how to sleep. To know how to sleep is not something you're born with; it's something you learn, something you gain, something you acquire, sometimes by hard work." Again I found myself asking, "What is this man talking about? Since I've been on this earth, I've been sleeping every night. I didn't have to learn it." He continued, "Initiation is about sleep. Knowing how to sleep. For if you don't know how to sleep, you won't know how to stay awake."

I was not really in the mood for rhetoric. I closed my eyes and went right back to sleep. I slept for two days.

When one has stayed awake for nine days, he knows what it means to be sleepy and fight sleepiness. When he goes to sleep, he experiences deep sleep. If he seeks wakefulness, then he may find wakefulness, for wakefulness can be reached only through the sleep of the just. This is something everyone can reach through practice, training, and exercise. Samnik let us sleep, knowing that we needed it; also knowing that it was a necessary step for him to reach his goal. Each time one of us woke up, he asked him to "go back to sleep, and be aware that you are awake while sleeping, or sleeping while awake."

I finally woke up for good. Some of my comrades were either trimming nets or studying cobwebs. Samnik asked me to join them. "After you trim a net," he told me, "untrim it. Pick a cobweb from the cave ceiling, and undo it. After you've undone it, put it back the way it was. Take your time. These exercises are absolutely necessary in order to set the mood for the knowledge that is to follow." He sat with me, trimmed a couple of nodes, untrimmed them, and trimmed them again. "Each time you trim a net," he explained, "you see how each node relates to all the nodes of the net. And each time you untie a node, you see how you destroy the whole net. It works the same for a cobweb."

"Pap, I understand the importance of nets," I said to him. "Fisherman use them to catch fish and feed their families. Hunters use them to catch animals. But what's the importance of cobwebs for us?"

"Fishermen catch only fish and hunters catch only animals, but spiders catch everything they need," he explained. "They have an edge on fishermen and hunters. We want you to narrow that edge."

To me, at the time, all this was ridiculous, but showing respect, I kept listening. "You'll stay awake only if you sleep and know how to sleep," the man continued. "You children are weary of traveling. But this trip called sleep is different. When you stay nine days without sleeping, you go to sleep, but in reality you take a journey. What you see and experience then is beautiful. Sometimes it's hard for you to come back here. Our world is so ugly. But at least you see. Yesterday, today, and tomorrow. Keep practicing. You won't need to stay awake a long period of time. You'll go and come at will.

"We have been together nearly a month now. I didn't have to decide to have you take this step; the whole clan decided it. Everyone who was born male in the village, your father, and his fathers before him, took this trip before you. They started the path; all they ask you to do is to stay on it and preserve it for those who come after you."

Here he stood up and called everybody's attention. "How in the world will you be able to keep the flame alive in your father's house if you don't stay awake? You were offered this chance to come, learn, and become men. You accepted the offer as you were supposed to do. Now you've come to the spider's house. Each moment counts. We have to stay here for the least possible time. We have no time to waste. If the master of this place comes back and finds us here, we are in trouble. He sees things that you don't see, hears things that you don't hear, knows things that you don't know as yet. Let's learn his craft and disappear before he shows up.

"It's not for you to go and teach others what you learn here. It's for you alone. Sleep now so that you stay awake forever. You reach your true nature only when you sleep. At that moment, you don't even yearn for the experience that others on the path have had.

"I'm telling you, there's nothing to teach. The only lesson worth giving or receiving is yourself, and the only book worth reading is nature. The path is serious. It's a source of deep joy. It's the most exciting adventure at the end of which is serenity. When you sleep and know how to free your true nature, the knowing springs forth. Your true nature is perfect and beyond comparison. This adventure that allows your true nature to come out, we call it Ngwey. Once, a group of boys to be initiated started to journey into Ngwey. Each night, they saw a river that they believed was Lom, a river we know around here. Loli Pakoo, their initiator, thought they went there to bathe, so every day he had to go looking for them, thinking that they had lost their sense of time. The truth was they went to the other shore, stealing other people's chickens and goats. Loli had to confront Lom, and Lom disappeared. That's the origin of the saying, 'Ngwey confronted Lom and Lom went underground.' This is to tell you the power of what we are doing here. But serenity is what the elders have asked me to lead you to. And the first step to serenity is net trimming. Trim nets."

The day we left the cave I recalled that my father had told me never to look back once I had chosen one path of life. So I kept my eyes on the road. I didn't really know if I had liked the cave, but I had had fun there. The most intense moment was reenacting the myth of the origins with my "brothers." Playing the part of the demiurges had given me a sense of greatness, an indescribable feeling of the value of life beyond what we ordinarily experience. Where were we going now? I didn't know. Someone asked this question but N'nenes gave him no reply. He enjoys placing us in situations for which we are not prepared, forcing us to come to terms and cope with them. Is this the best way to understand the nature and meaning of everything that happens to us now and hereafter?

N'nenes woke us at 8 the last morning. "Pack," he ordered, "we're going home." As each boy finished packing, N'nenes took him by the hand to the river. When my turn came, he took me also by the hand and we headed for the river. I could see my father waiting on the other shore. N'nenes hugged me and pressed my ear to his heart. "What do you hear, boy?"

"I hear a voice calling me by name," I replied, "Me, Nouk, son of Bian, son of Bassomb, son of Batama, son of Nsom, son of Bixok, son of Njem, son of Bian, son of Hisee, son of Koti, son of Ngon, son of Gwek, son of Kooy, son of Ndombi, son of Gwaxoo, son of Mode, son of Sop, son of Manal, son of Mban, son of the Rock. It's telling me that I have been born anew, coming from the Rock, which is the mother, to the forest, which is her womb. In the forest, the night is a friend. And everything that sees. The voice is telling me that Koba, son of Hilolombi the Creator, didn't wait for anyone to tell him what to do. Compassion was enough; that's why we call him Ngookola, 'Compassion-was-enough.' To see is a path that kills or heals. I chose to heal and save. But I can kill and destroy. I am the anointed one. The anointed one is a healer and savior—the one who takes his people to safety. I am Nanga, son of the Rock."

"Go on, son," cried Samnik, "tell me things as they come to you. Don't worry if the tongue fails; you have all your life to develop the knowing, to discover the hidden, to see the unseen. Tell me!"

"The voice is telling me to trim a net. Trim a net, it's telling me. And don't worry if others untrim it. I've got to keep trimming, and build a network of friends here and in the spirit world. To heal is to unfold the mind backward to its perfection, then forward again to its predictability. This life is linear. It is also circular and cyclical. Its cyclical nature causes it to be predictable. Life is a succession of nows and heres that unfold in a predictable way. The initiate makes sure his mind moves forward in harmony with life's successions. That's how he keeps chaos from occurring again. Difficulties are best solved before they arise. The mind is all power. It's the net that catches everything. Everything comes from it; everything goes back into it."

"Go now, boy, your father is waiting."

I crossed the river and hugged my father. He too pressed my ear to his heart. "What do you hear, son?" he asked me. "What do you hear?"

I repeated what I had told Samnik and added, "The father is the one who engenders as well as the one who raises a child, but the son is the one who corrects his father's mistakes. If the father is drunk, he takes him to bed; if he is naked, he covers him. Hilolombi the Creator had the right to make mistakes. He had the right to punish the multitude for the deeds of one man. His twin sons Koba and Kwan also had the right to stay put, to do nothing, to laugh at their Father and the world, but Koba decided that he would come to our rescue. He is blessed for that. The voice tells me that the succession of our lineage must be assured and that in the house my father built the fire must always continue to burn."

He smiled and took me to the center of the village. The tom-tom was beating, and N'nenes' circumcision knife was already glowing red-hot in the fire.

GOOD-BYE, MOTHER

WANDER PIROLI

© Wilson Avelar

W ander Piroli was born in Brazil in 1931. He received a law degree from the Federal University of Mina Gerais, but subsequently abandoned his law practice in favor of a full-time career as a journalist and writer.

Mr. Piroli is the author of three collections of short stories and two young-adult novels. In 1982, he was awarded First Prize by the São Paulo Foundation of Art Critics and the Premio Jabuti from the Association of Brazilian Book Publishers for his novel *Os rios morrem de sede*. Mr. Piroli's short stories have also appeared in anthologies published in English, French, German, Italian, Polish, Portuguese, Russian, and Spanish. The following selection is from the collection *O Moderno Conto Brasileiro* (The Modern Brazilian Short Story).

Mr. Piroli makes his home in Brazil. He is married and has four children.

Mother is stretched out on the pantry table. A white sheet covers her, covers the whole table. Aunt Mafalda is standing by the table with her stubborn face of stone. The room is empty, and six empty chairs line the wall. Aunt Mafalda knows that I am here. I am leaning against the kitchen door, my jacket under my arm.

"Aunt Mafalda."

She slowly turns her face of stone, and seeing me without looking at me, lifts her hand to silence me. Now she begins to move in my direction.

"Lavinia is asleep."

She nears, she pushes me to the side, she passes.

"Mother is dead."

"I want to show you something, Luiz."

I follow her to the backyard. She points at a mound of red earth under a trellised grapevine. A grave.

"It's for Lavinia."

"Aunt Mafalda!"

"This is where Lavinia will stay."

"Mother has to be taken to the cemetery."

"It is her wish to stay here."

"You know that she cannot."

Aunt Mafalda almost smiles. A smile that is not in the least disdainful.

"Who dug the grave?"

"The two of us."

"Mother too?"

"Yes."

"But wasn't she ill?"

"She was before."

"Did Mother know she was dying?"

"She always knew."

"When did it happen?"

"The day before yesterday, at night."

"So it's been two days."

"She wanted you to come."

"I can't believe that."

Irritated, she glares at me.

"Lavinia dictated the telegram."

"Aunt Mafalda."

"Come, let's go, Luiz. Lavinia is all alone."

We pass the cistern, the kitchen, we are again in the empty room.

Did no one come?

Aunt Mafalda grips the sheet and uncovers Mother's face. The same fanatical face as five years ago. The same black scarf to hide the repulsive baldness.

"Kiss her."

"There's no point, Aunt Mafalda."

"Luiz. Kiss her."

"Please stop it."

"Quickly, Luiz."

I look into the face of stone.

"Lavinia is waiting, Luiz!"

I lean over Mother. She is opening her eyes. I pull back. I try to back away, but Aunt Mafalda grasps my hand.

"Come on, Luiz."

"I can't."

Aunt Mafalda's voice is hoarse, hoarse like my mother's voice:

"Come here, my boy."

I bend down over the table. Aunt Mafalda pushes me down by the nape until she is sure my mouth touches my mother's withered cheek.

"Right, Luiz."

"Mother is still warm."

"Yes."

"Did you not say that she died the day before yester-day?"

"Lavinia was waiting for you."

Aunt Mafalda covers Mother's face with the sheet.

"Now help me."

She takes the body at one end, and I at the other. Mother weighs almost nothing. We carry her through the kitchen, past the cistern, and to the trellised grapevine. We place the body at the side of the grave. Aunt Mafalda ties a rope around Mother's legs. We lower her, one end at a time.

"It's all right, Luiz"—Aunt Mafalda drives a shovel into the red earth—"You can go now."

As I go through the kitchen, I hear the dampened sound of earth falling onto Mother's body. I cross the bare pantry, the corridor, the porch. I push forward so as not to see Mother and Aunt Mafalda by the old wicker chairs.

Translated from the Portuguese
by Peter Constantine

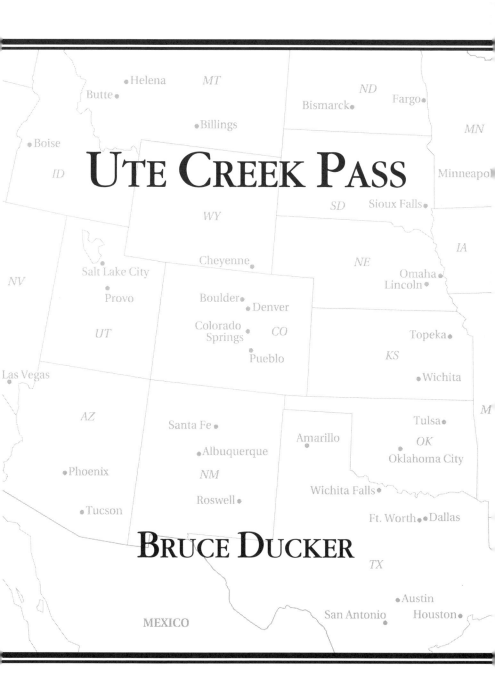

UTE CREEK PASS

BRUCE DUCKER

Bruce Ducker was born in New York City in 1938. He received a bachelor's degree from Dartmouth and both a master's and a law degree from Columbia University. He has had a private law practice since 1964.

Mr. Ducker is the author of several books, including *Rule by Proxy, Failure at the Mission Trust*, and *Bankroll*. His novel *Marital Assets* was nominated for the Pulitzer Prize in literature, and his most recent book, *Lead Us Not into Penn Station*, has been nominated by the American Library Association as a Best Book for 1994. Mr. Ducker's writing has been featured in several publications including the *Yale Review, New York Quarterly*, and *Commonweal*.

Mr. Ducker lives in Denver with his wife, Jaren. They have three children.

They drove south out of Cheyenne. He looked at the sky, gray and soggy, and wished they weren't going.

"Could get rained on."

"Could happen," Craig said. Then later, "Sometimes it brings the fish up."

"Sometimes." He didn't think so, though. Sometimes it put the fish down. More often than not. One thing he knew: It would be cold and wet.

He would not have thought of going if Helen hadn't pushed him. Pushed him out the door. Do you good. Helen always knew what would do him good. Get out for the day. Remember how he used to love to go fishing with you?

He remembered. It was ages ago, when Craig was ten, eleven. Craig could fish all day. They would pack into Wind Rivers, into the Medicine Bow Range, fish the Encampment, the North Platte. Craig wouldn't quit until it was too dark to see the fly. Lord, that was a long time ago.

"How far you figure this place is, Dad?"

"Three and a half, maybe four hours. A long way to go for the day."

"We could stay over. I remember a motel in Hot Sulphur Springs." Craig had a road map spread across his knees, and his finger was tracing a route.

"Can't. Got to be at work tomorrow." He didn't mean it as a rebuke, although the words sounded harsh as they left his mouth. Craig had no work, no regular work. He got by. Just now he drove a truck for a firm in Tucson, when he wanted to. He and his girlfriend seemed not to need steady work to make a go of it, if you'd call the way they lived making a go of it. He wouldn't. No order, no regularity.

Can't live on nachos and love, he had told Helen, and

she had said, Ed Berry, you old tree. Can't you remember what it was like?

Sure he could. He remembered he always liked clean sheets on the bed and fresh vegetables and knowing he was expected places. If that's what Helen meant, yes he could remember. If she meant being young meant being something else, no, he didn't remember that.

Why Craig was studying the map was a mystery. Ed knew the way well enough. Down into Colorado, where the fishing couldn't be as good as it was just twenty miles north of Cheyenne, then across the Divide and pick up the Colorado River at Granby. Seemed a long way to drive. Man Ed knew, more of a customer than a friend, had invited him down. Man leased out rights on his ranch through September to some oil men in Denver. Now he had the rights back, and kept telling Ed how it was great fishing. At least, sometimes. 'Course, he wasn't a fisherman himself.

Damn fool is probably wrong, thought Ed. Probably knows as little about fishing as he knows about balers. Man paid too damn much for every piece of equipment he had bought from Ed since they'd known each other.

"Sky may be opening up, Dad."

Sure enough, in the west a cleaved wedge of blue. Like someone took a slice out of a peach, to see if it was ready for eating.

"May be."

The drive was too long but easy. They had taken the Scout. Not that they needed it, but the whole idea of having a four-wheel drive was that it was Ed's car. For fishing and hunting. He liked that, he liked packing it with the gear, the waders, the long tubes for the fly rods, the hats—his old felt and Craig's, kind of a leather, hippie thing with a wide brim and a feather. Helen made sandwiches and stacked them, each neatly squared away in a plastic bag with the flap folded in and the sleeve pulled over, in an orderly column in the Igloo. Cans of diet pop for Ed, regular for Craig, chips, cole slaw, an apple each, and a nut bar.

They had risen before dawn and had taken a large breakfast. By the time he'd been driving an hour, thinking of what Helen had sent along, Ed was hungry.

"Reach back there, Craig, and get me an apple."

His son hooked a long arm over into the rear seat and flipped open the cooler. He found an apple, took it from its little plastic bag and shined it on the whitened knee of his jeans. From deep in the pocket of his chamois shirt, he pulled out a knife and used his teeth to open its blade. Then he neatly halved the apple and with what seemed one motion removed the seeds and core.

He passed over the half to his father, offering it balanced on the tips of his fingers.

Ed felt better as he ate. Craig bit into the other half. Ain't that something, Ed thought. He's going to eat my half. Later on, if I want more apple, well, I'll have to eat his half. Isn't that an ass-backwards way of doing things, when we both start out with our own apple.

They were too late for the colors. The leaves of aspen and cottonwood turn and fall early in the mountains, and all the gold had gone by mid-September. Maybe south. Maybe there would be some color left down in the San Luis, where Ed used to go every autumn to shoot geese. The San Luis Valley, with its wide, glacier-forced floor, its marshes, its tiny streams that fed into the Arkansas, the Rio Grande, the Saguache. Ed loved that valley. 'Course, there was good bird country close to home. In the flyway of the Big Horn north of Sheridan, geese and duck were plentiful. No question, though, the country to the south was beautiful. If he didn't love it so, he would never drive the extra hours. Too far, too many people. Besides, he didn't like Coloradoans. Seemed as if every time he'd see one of their damn green license plates, it was where it wasn't supposed to be, hadn't asked permission, had taken up in a hole he liked to fish. Too many of them. They've ruined their damned state, now they're going to ruin mine.

"Lord, what country."

Craig's words brought his eyes off the highway. It was true. They were coming across Trail Ridge Road, over twelve thousand feet. The snowpack from last winter had not melted off completely, and you could see layers like a fancy pastry where the new snows this fall had already settled. Bleached, dormant grasses stretched back from the snows to the peaks in the distance. Craig pulled out the thermos from the rear seat and poured two cups of coffee. Ed took his and breathed in its steam. The air smelled of sage and frost.

"Some country, huh, Dad."

His father nodded. "Some country," he said moments later.

"It's sure been great to get this week at home. Mollie and I have talked about getting you and Mom down to Tucson, but I told her, If I wanted to see you during bird season, I'd better make the trip down here."

"Not shooting so much any more."

"No? Why not?"

"Don't know," Ed said. "Doesn't seem as much fun anymore. Shot a lot of birds over the years. We have a locker full of dove and duck. Won't go hungry."

Craig laughed. "Really." Craig had this way of saying Really, the way the kids do today, when they mean right, or I understand. Ed didn't like it.

There were reasons about the hunting, but he kept them to himself. It was true that the fun had gone out of it. For one thing his hunting buddy had quit. Man was just sixty and he'd developed palsy. Or whatever they were calling it now. Didn't think he should be handling a loaded shotgun, shaking like someone in a home. Besides, Ed thought, I've tired of the blood. The feathers, the dead eyes, the blood. I've shot a lot of birds.

Craig let it go. He was on to something else. What color he and Mollie painted the walls and where they wanted to go in January and whether you were better off with a gas range or electric. Craig was like his mother. Never lacked for talk.

They rolled through Granby. At the far end of town they stopped for gas and bought one-day licenses at a shanty store that sold T-shirts, salmon eggs, and home-made beef jerky by the register. Back on the road, they picked up the Colorado River as it ran west. From here it flowed across the state, through Glenwood Springs and down through dams and canyons into the Sea of Cortez. All that water dumping into a Mexican ocean and ranchers in Wyoming thirsting for it.

It was close to eleven when they found the turn-off past Parshall. Craig jumped out to open the wire gate and got back in after the car rolled over the cattle guard. A jeep road, rutted and splotched with cow pies, jogged down to a grove of cottonwoods. Ed steered the Scout in among them and turned off the motor.

"Raining," he said.

"Not too bad. A drizzle."

Craig was right. They got out and put on their waders, rain jackets, vests. Hard by them, beyond the grove of trees, ran the river, black as rock.

"No hatch on."

"Not yet," Craig said. "How 'bout we eat now? Then we can fish straight through."

They sat in the light rain, he on the car fender, Craig cross-legged on the damp ground, on its blanket of leaves and dust. They set the cooler between them and put their pop cans on it. Ed watched the river and saw nothing. On the opposite bank, an ouzel hopped about on the rocks searching for bugs.

They decided to split up. Ed walked downstream and

Craig up. They were to meet at the car at four if they didn't see each other before.

At first he fished hard. There were no hatches and no fish fed on the surface. And so he fished deeper, drifting a nymph then a wet fly to find the deep-lying trout, free-drifting it as if it had just jarred loose from its pupal shuck attached to the riverbed stones. People put nymphing down—the dry-fly purists put it down—but it took more skill, more intuition. You had to feel that fish mouth the nymph, sense when the line veered or stopped for the briefest moment, and strike before the fish spit out the tiny lure. It was a skill, and a lot of people fished for years before they picked it up and a lot more never got it at all.

So he concentrated and fished hard, but in three hours he found only two fish, both browns, spotted red and silver with golden bellies shining in the faint October light. It was as if the fish were the source, not the sky, the source of the light. He netted each fish, then he slipped out the hook, righted the trout in the water and let it go. The fish swam off slowly, without fear, and swam out of his sight and out of the memory of the encounter. By the time it disappeared under the stream's moss beds it was again a wild thing.

Now he had waded upstream to where the car was. He was chilled from the river and the constant mist. He took off his waders and vest, got in the driver's door, and turned on the heater. He leaned back and lowered the headrest so it bolstered the base of his skull. The warm air blew through the fan belt and he could feel the dampness melt from his leggings and his wool shirt.

He woke. He reached briefly, urgently, for his dream—it was an important one—but he couldn't bring it back. Where had he been? Had he been younger? Stronger? It would not return.

Again he put on the clothes of his pursuit. Now he walked upstream, to see what new riffles and pools the river held.

The rain had stopped and the clouds seemed to have come together. They made distinct forms now, hanging lower and bellied with rain. Rays of the sun bounced among their forms, and while he sensed light through the seams of the clouds, there were no shadows.

Around an oxbow bend, beyond the willows, he saw his son. Craig stood erect in midstream, the river low about his thighs, watching his flyline. Like an osprey will watch a feeding fish. When it falters, when it hesitates, he moves. The fly went through its perfect drift, and Craig rolled out line with a swift push of his rod, into an elegant serpentine above his head, and allowed another cast to float onto the water's surface.

Thinking like a fish isn't enough, he had taught him. You have to be that river bed and those stones and that mayfly nymph, sweeping down in the current. You have to see that trout pick you out, leave his feeding station, slowly sip you in. Then you strike.

Ed watched the boy for an hour. Craig caught several fish. Some good size. Each one he played from the reel with a look in his eye that Ed recognized.

Cannot believe he'd want to leave Cheyenne, Ed thought. Much as he loves this country. Good a fisherman as he is. He remembered the arguments about Craig's quitting high school. How he didn't want to work in Ed's office or out back, in the yard. You'd think most kids would love that job, driving tractors and backhoes and doing things that most kids dream about doing. Some things, Ed thought, I just won't understand. Helen had said, You got to let him go, so he let him go. And now what he had was a kid who lived in Arizona, who could fish like that, and nothing to show for the years but wonderment about what he hadn't done right.

They agreed that the clouds looked ominous and that, with the low flicker of lightning beyond the rim of the land, they ought to move along. Craig had the map out as Ed stowed the last of the gear into the boot of the wagon.

"Look here, Dad. See that road? Looks like it can save us time."

Craig was right. A dirt road, bearing a state highway number, cut a diagonal across the perpendicular route they had used that morning.

"Don't know. Might be a jeep road."

"I don't think so, Dad. I mean, it's a state highway, and here on the key they list jeep roads dotted, not solid. Looks driveable. Ute Creek Pass. What say? Want to try it?"

"Could just as soon cost us time as make it up."

"Could. Still, we're in no rush, and it's a new way to go. Let's give it a try. I'll drive, if you want."

Ed glanced at the gathering dark. Beams of sun snuck through the clouds like reef fish and swam to earth. What the hell, he thought. That's what the Scout is for.

He handed Craig the keys. "Let's give it a try."

The turn was well marked by a sign.

UTE CREEK PASS
SUMMIT 19 MILES

Ed figured if they did even half the speed on the pass, they'd cut some time off the return trip. Nineteen miles to the summit, another fifteen miles down. He didn't want to be on that road when they lost the last glow of dusk. Funny feeling to have your kid drive you. Ed had never been a passenger in the Scout.

The road snaked up a long, easy rise. After five miles, the pavement stopped, and they were on gravel. Then the gravel gave out, and it was bladed dirt, red and hard-packed, the marl slick under the headlights of the climbing Scout. No cars, no signs, no evidence that the road led anywhere but into the balconies of heaven.

They hadn't spoken since the turn-off. Ed began to won-

der if this was such a good idea. A breakdown, for
instance. You could slide off the road and snap a connect-
ing rod, and who the hell was there to help them? At the
point of no return, a three-hour walk back to nowhere.
This was a damn foolhardy idea, and he was angry that
he'd let himself be talked into it.

They climbed, passing patches of ponderosa. Through
the trees was cut an occasional timbering path, and the
trails made Ed brighten that perhaps all civilization was
not behind them. The evening light came across the land
low and bright, like a filtered spotlight. In the rays of one
of those lights, Ed saw a sign by the roadside.

UTE CREEK PASS SUMMIT 6 MI.
TABERNASH MINE 6 MI.

"Did you see that, Dad?" Craig sounded relieved. Ed
took some comfort that Craig too was rethinking the route
they had chosen. "Did you see that? What do you suppose
they're mining up here?"

"Don't know," said Ed. "I never heard of no mining up
here."

Both men now leaned forward in the car. Craig pushed
the speed a little, drifting around one curve on the wet dirt
and sending a chill to Ed's groin. The sky was backlit, the
last band of light only now being forced out of existence
by the clouds of settling rain.

The engine labored at the higher altitudes. They had
come up several thousand feet from the river. Not as high
as Trail Ridge, but the car seemed to rear and pitch. Every
time it slipped down a gear the car lurched, and with
every lurch Ed swore to himself it would be the last auto-
matic transmission he'd buy. Fine for a woman's car. But if
he was going to have a mountain car, damn it, it would
have a standard shift. This was a three-legged horse.

They came around another serpentine turn, rod cases

119

rolling noisily in the back, and there at the head of a moraine stood the damnedest sight Ed had ever seen. In the middle of nowhere, at the top of a Colorado mountain pass, a four-story building with three giant stacks coming out of it. Surrounding the building was a hurricane fence twelve feet high, all lit up as if it were a ball field for a night game. The mill was set in the hollow of a mountain peak that had been scooped out like a cantaloupe. What was missing wasn't fruit, but rock blasted free and rolled and crushed for extraction. On either side of the building were long, rectangular settling ponds, dammed and still, each the size of a football field, each shimmering green and electric as a tourmaline.

"My God," said Craig.

Ed said nothing. They drove the few hundred yards to the plant's main gate. The road passed right by it. Craig braked the car to a halt and looked out.

"What in hell do you suppose it is?"

"Right there," said Ed. There was a metal sign on the gate with black lettering.

TABERNASH MINE AND MILL
UTE CREEK PASS
INTERNATIONAL METALS CORP.
NO TRESPASSING

Ed had rolled down his window to get a better look. A voice split across the loudspeaker and startled them both.

"Help you fellows?"

They peered in. Behind the gate, under the only overhead light that was not trained on the plant, stood a man in a yellow hardhat. In his hand he held a microphone the size of a grenade. It hooked up to a black conical speaker mounted on the top of the gate.

"No. Just looking."

"Fine." He turned to walk away.

"Ask him what they mine, Dad."

"Don't be a damn fool, Craig. None of our business."

"Go ahead. Ask him."

Ed swallowed. "Say, . . ."

The man turned.

"What do you all mine here?"

"Molybdenum."

"That right?" Ed said. He turned to Craig. "Molybdenum."

"Damn," said Craig.

Ed rolled up his window and, as if in concert, they looked forward and Craig drove away.

The trip down the east side of the pass was uneventful.

"Molybdenum," said Craig as they rejoined the paved highway. "What the hell is molybdenum?"

"Use it for steel. Use it in the making of steel."

"That place, Dad. It looked like it could have been in Russia or somewhere. Know what I mean?"

"I do," said Ed. "It could have been in the Himalayas or someplace like that."

"Really. Coming on that in the middle of nowhere and all. Wasn't that something?"

Ed agreed that it was something. He didn't speak any words, but he nodded and in the darkness Craig knew he had.

They descended the pass, saying little. The sequence of road surfaces was reversed—the bladed dirt road, then gravel, then pavement and they knew they were close to the highway. At the spot where the two roads again joined, there was a convenience store with two gas pumps.

"You going to feel like eating before we get home?" Ed asked.

"Whatever you like. Maybe we can grab something for the car."

They parked and went into the store. It was empty except for the woman behind the counter. She was reading

Screenplay. In front of her a small portable black-and-white television set with an enormous aerial was broadcasting a quiz show.

"Howdy," said Ed.

"Evening."

"Cold," said Craig, rubbing his hands.

"Not yet," she said and smiled. She was Ed's age, maybe older, a big woman with bushy gray hair. She wore a heavy ribbed cardigan sweater over a flannel shirt and jeans.

"Got anything hot to eat?"

"I can heat you up some sandwiches," she said. "In the nuker. And there's coffee."

Ed looked at Craig.

"Sounds just right," he said.

They returned to the Scout with a paper bag full of food and a six-pack of Coors. Ed drove, while Craig handed him his dinner. He took a can of beer and propped it between his thighs, and with his left hand on the wheel took what Craig offered. They ate chili dogs, and potato chips, and french fries in a cardboard dish shaped like the boats Ed used to make from newspaper for Craig and the girls when they were kids. It rained heavily as they ate, but they had dried off from the stream and the Scout's heater hummed under the dash.

"Dad?"

"Um?"

"Mind if I ask you something?"

"No. 'Course not."

"Why'd you and Mom get married? I mean, how did you decide you wanted to?"

"Well," Ed said. He licked salt from his fingertips.

"Well, the usual reasons. You know."

Craig was silent, and Ed thought a minute.

"I mean, we loved each other and wanted to be together. And of course it wasn't like now. You didn't live together."

"Did you have girlfriends before Mom?"

Ed smiled. "Yeah. Sure. I mean, one or two serious ones."

"Ones that you slept with?"

"Yeah. That too. Sex was around then, too." Ed smiled, and he looked over to see Craig.

"I just mean, how do you know you want to marry one and not the other?"

Ed let some highway go by.

"You thinking of getting married?"

"No," Craig said quickly. "But you know, Mollie and I talk about it and all. You know how women are."

"Sure. I guess we did too. Well, your mother and I kind of lived together, but not in the open. And if you wanted to have kids and everything, well, we thought we ought to get married."

A semi hauling two trailers of cattle came at them. Through the tires Ed felt the rumbling of the truck as it passed and as it moved away from them. Rain streaked the windshield and the night surrounded them.

"Did you want to have kids?"

"Can't say as how I'd really thought it through. Your mother did, and it sounded OK to me." He drank the last sip of beer, turned warm from the heat of his body, and handed Craig the empty can.

"Another?"

"Not yet. Don't want to make a piss stop in this weather."

They rode for a while in the quiet.

"Well, what do you think of it?" Craig asked.

"Of what?"

"Marriage."

Ed took a breath. He hadn't thought of it, at least not for a while.

"Well. It's been different."

"What do you mean?"

"Different from what I thought. I guess I thought it'd be having your best friend sleep over all the time. But it's been different. More complicated."

"How so?"

"With kids and all. Don't get me wrong. We wanted all you kids, you and your sisters. But it sure takes energy. I don't think I knew anything about it. It just changes your life, and you don't know it's coming."

Craig seemed to ponder that. Ed wasn't satisfied with it, but it was all he could say.

"We got cinnamon twists and jelly doughnuts."

"A twist," said Ed. "And another beer. Can't eat jelly doughnuts and steer."

"Want me to drive?"

"Nah. We're an hour out. No more."

Ed ate the pastry. It left his hands sticky, and he gathered the dew from the fresh can of beer to wash them. They would be out of the mountains soon and he could pick up Cheyenne on the radio.

"Damn," said Craig.

"What's that?"

"Sex sure is a strong thing."

Ed nodded. "Sure is."

The road passed into a flat part, and they moved faster across the open range. There was an occasional car now, and with each one that crossed there was a flick of bright lights and the shudder of air as they passed.

Now the rain came mixed with snow against the windshield, hard to tell apart, and Ed edged the heater up a notch. As it grew colder, the snow might start to stick, and the driving would get tricky. But if that happened, he didn't notice. Soon they were out of the hills, the flakes and raindrops keeping an equilibrium, and he was turning north toward home.

*   *   *

The next morning he was surprised to hear voices in the kitchen. Craig hadn't been up for breakfast since he'd arrived. He had noticed: It rankled him to leave for work every morning while his son slept through and his wife waited to fix another breakfast. But this morning, as he stood shaving in the bathroom at the top of the stairs, he heard the voices of Helen and Craig in the kitchen. He hurried to join them.

"You'd have to see it," Craig was saying. "It was like a sci-fi movie or something. Wasn't it, Dad?"

"What's that, Craig?"

"The mine. The Tabernash Mine."

"Yeah. It was something to see."

"I guess," Craig agreed. "Like another planet. Out in the middle of nowhere, Ma. A sci-fi movie."

"That must have been something to see," said Helen. "How come you didn't mention it?"

Ed shrugged. He poured himself a cup of coffee from the Pyrex pot and sat down at the kitchen table. Helen put a glass of juice and a plate with two slices of toast and bacon in front of him.

"I asked your father about the trip," Helen said to Craig. "You want to know what he said?"

"What?" Craig and Helen were looking at each other in complicity, getting ready to laugh.

"Not many fish." They laughed and Helen repeated what Ed had said.

"That's true," said Ed. "Not many fish."

"It was a good trip, though," Craig said.

Ed looked at him and nodded. He chewed his toast slowly. When he had finished and had drunk his coffee, he looked at his watch.

"Damn. The time. Got to go." He rose and left in a rush, although it was the time he always left for work, even a little early.

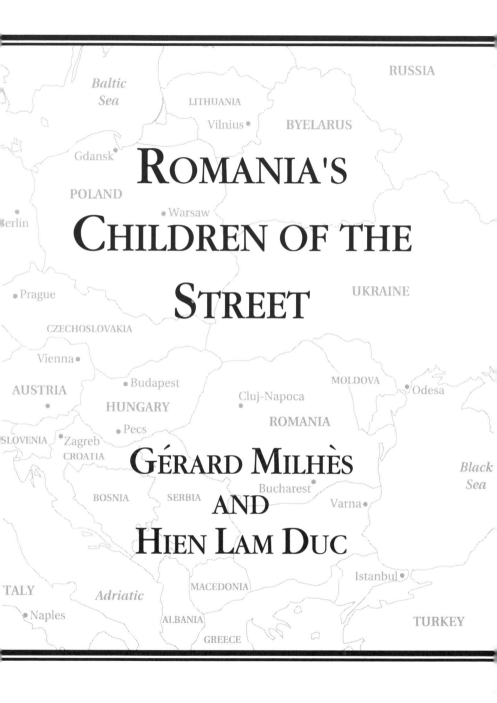

ROMANIA'S
CHILDREN OF THE
STREET

GÉRARD MILHÈS
AND
HIEN LAM DUC

Gérard Milhès was born in Toulouse, France, in 1953. He earned a degree in psychology, then worked in industry and founded a radio station. He became an educator for deaf and blind children and assisted in a remedial education program for sixteen- to twenty-five-year-olds. He was head of finance at the Association of Media and Audiovisual Communication and a journalist for *Lyon-Liberation*. He is currently editor-in-chief of *A Presence in the World*, published by ONG ÉquiLibre, a humanitarian organization.

Hien Lam Duc was born in Laos in 1964. His childhood was marked by frequent uprooting, prison, refugee camps, and invasions as a result of war in Indochina. His schooling was sporadic. In 1977, he arrived in France, earned an undergraduate degree, and became a free-lance photographer. A fashion photographer in the late 1980s, he returned to Laos in 1989 to prepare a story on the Ho Chi Minh trail. In 1990 and 1992, he documented human rights conditions worldwide for ÉquiLibre.

Messrs. Milhès and Lam Duc traveled to Romania twice for ÉquiLibre. The following selection is excerpted from their book *Roumanie: Les gamins du pave* (Romania: The Kids of the Street) and from *Graines d'Hommes* (Seeds of Man), edited by Patrick Bernard.

February freezes the streets and the wind whips the piles of snow. The icy city of Bucharest flirts with subfreezing temperatures. In the courtyard of the North Train Station a statue of two mustachioed Romanian railroad heroes stands impassive. At its base a few abandoned children seek protection from the polar night around a fire built of cardboard boxes. The voice of a gypsy mingles with the flames. His powerful melody carries the nostalgia of the Balkans. "Little Sister in Purple," the tragic ballad speaks of sorrow and wasted love.

The singer's name is Mugurel. His father, a guitarist, left him with musical talent as well as multiple fractures of the skull at his brow and temple. "At home I was beaten all the time, so the spring that holds my thoughts together bursts and I get crazy."

Having fled from his brutal family, Mugurel has lived on the streets of Bucharest for two years. Born in the village of Dacia, near Brasov, the twelve-year-old child who looks more like ten hardly knew his parents. He was placed in an orphanage at the age of six months and lived there seven years. There he was roughly taught that might makes right. He was fed meager broth, poorly clothed, and supervised by older children who stole his food, put paper between his toes and set it on fire, drove wooden splinters under his fingernails, and raped him while he slept. His favorite childhood memory is of the neuropsychiatric hospital. "I felt good there, I was well fed."

Less than a year after being returned to his family, Mugurel, too often abused, left for good.

Like dozens of young runaways, he found lodging at the North Train Station, where he begs by imitating a one-legged person. When this dodge does not meet his needs, he goes on a tour of the university, where he steals students'

money and calculators. But sometimes the toughest battle in this glacial winter is staking out a warm place to sleep next to a waiting room radiator and avoiding the police.

When it is warm out and he has eaten and hasn't had any scuffles, Mugurel returns to being a child armed with a squirt gun, or mimicking an obese taxi driver gorging on fatback and cabbage, scratching his belly the while.

After a trip to the movies where he goes for his "good entertainment" of martial arts films from Korea, Mugurel laughs until he cries, recounting the exploits of the golden Ninja. He becomes mischievous, eyes flashing, using all his charm to win what he misses the most, a gentle touch.

An adolescent with black hair and scarred face pulls from her pocket a gold-colored plastic bag half filled with a sticky liquid. She puts her lips around the opening and deeply inhales the vapor that will soon make her hilarious.

Every day Stella gets high on the fumes of lacquer aerosol, a glazing compound inhaled by the children of the streets. "Lacquer aerosol is stronger than alcohol. When I get high I feel like I'm falling; I'm afraid the sky is going to

fall on my head. That's when I go and hide in the bushes. I go through two bottles a day. That way I'm never hungry."

All the street kids enact this ritual. "The drug takes away all my feelings of hunger, cold, and fear." Under the influence of the methyl benzene in the lacquer, Stella swings her head and arms, acts like a kitten, and screams—all the while hurling abusive language at the adults who pass by giving her disapproving glances. Her eyes are vague and lost.

Stella is fifteen. She survives by virtue of a few housewives who give her handouts and the florists who pay her to bring them water. Her behavior while high ranges from foolishly insulting adults who had momentarily wanted to help her to endlessly complaining about her miserable existence. When she emerges from these fogs, she expresses concern about the children who are even worse off. "I pity them sleeping on cement or in garbage cans. I did the same thing and ended up in the hospital," she says.

Slender and slight, afraid of nothing and nobody, Costel stands nearby with an American cigarette hanging out of his mouth. Lame, he is unable to outrun the police. At ten

he is a veteran of the train station. He says he's been living there for three years. He regrets nothing. "My mother, I never see her, I don't miss her. It's too late for me to go to school. I don't know how to read, but too bad! I know how to count, and nobody can cheat me." He wants to be a businessman.

Unlike the other young vagabonds, who hang out in groups, Costel prefers to live and work alone. And Costel does work: He is a newspaper vendor. When the opportunity presents itself, he plays one of the most popular sports at the train station: stealing newspapers from mail carts destined for the outskirts of Romania. But Costel does not steal often. Ordinarily, he buys his stacks of *Azi* or *Libertatea* at half price from Cellophane, his mail service contact at the train station. Cellophane augments his own meager postal salary by misappropriating bundles of daily papers. Costel resells them at a profit to other children, who in turn sell them in the station. "I always have money," boasts Costel, treating two of his buddies to a bag of popcorn. Some days he earns the equivalent of the minimum wage. And to banish all doubt, he pulls out a nice bundle of bills.

The Bucharest police arrest street children regularly and transfer them to a sorting-out center, a depot from which they are dispersed to orphanages. Paul has been locked up in a center for ninety days. He comes from the country-side, near Tulcea at the mouth of the Danube. Puny, his white skin tinged with gray, he does not look his thirteen years. He speaks with his head lowered, concealing the embarrassment and sadness evident in his large eyes. His restless hands clutch the chair. He could no longer tolerate the orphanage where his mother had placed him. "Mama never visited me. The older kids knocked me around, stealing my meals." So one night, Paul fled in the company of three accomplices.

They escaped to Constanta. For a while they lived off the leftovers from the train station buffet, offered by a mother-ly waitress. But after three days the police ordered them to move along or they would be arrested. Paul boarded a train, and his travels began again. To Bucharest, of course, where he escaped a police roundup, but also to Buzau, Ploiesti, and Slobozia. Not liking to beg, Paul occasionally found work harvesting watermelons or picking corn. This

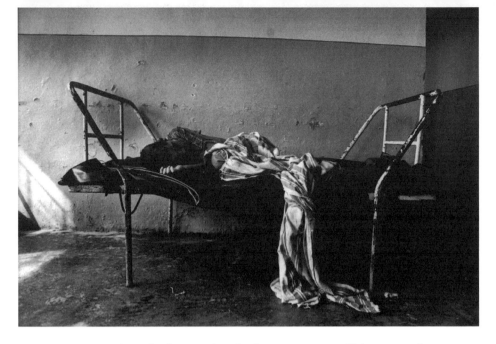

summer interlude remains the best memory of his escapade.

But inevitably, Paul returned to the North Train Station. "I didn't like living there. Other kids forced me to go steal with them. I was afraid. The worst thing was the cold. I was so dirty, infested with bugs." Rubbing his groin, still painful after a hernia operation, the sad child bravely imagines his future. "I would have wanted to return to my mother's house. But in the three months that I've been here, she hasn't thought it worthwhile to come and get me. Now I'm sure that she no longer wants me. It would be nice to learn a trade. I don't know what's going to happen to me. Say! I sure hope I can get something out of life."

These are the sons and daughters born of the demented politics of Nicolae Ceausescu. The Romanian dictator rose to power in 1967, and in the same year the birth rate law was enacted. The leader decided to strengthen Romania by doubling the population, making it a nation of fifty million inhabitants. To achieve that demographic objective, each woman was required to bear five children for her country. Women suspected of having an abortion risked

several years in prison, and doctors who performed abortions could be imprisoned for seven years. The only abortions permitted were to women past the age of forty-five and women who had already borne five children. A sort of gynecological police evolved. In the workplace women were examined every two months until a pregnancy was confirmed.

Before his fall and execution in 1989, Ceausescu's determination to augment the population was responsible for the birth of thousands of children in the impoverished country. Meanwhile, to satisfy the dictator's nationalistic goal of paying off Romania's foreign debt, Romania sold everything it had to sell. Train after train loaded with food supplies were sent to the Soviet Union. For the hungry Romanian people it was a time of misery.

Desperate mothers placed children they did not want or could not feed into orphanages. To house these children, institutions sprang up everywhere, but lack of government financial support condemned them to a cold and malnourished childhood. Adults too were suffering extreme want, and the situation of the orphans did not

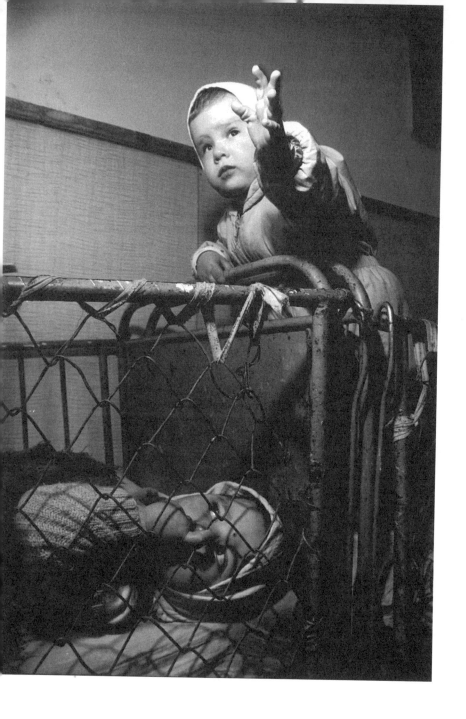

escape them. Often absolute despots reigned over homes for orphans, where beatings were more frequent than meals. Older children robbed the younger ones, beat them, and forced them to perform sexual acts. The orphans' parents, submerged in their daily struggle against hunger, soon forgot them. By the thousands, these abandoned children grew up deprived of affection and basic kindness. During the revolution they spilled into the streets, escaping the orphanages where their shattered youth was spent.

Translated from the French
by Jeanne Strazzabosco

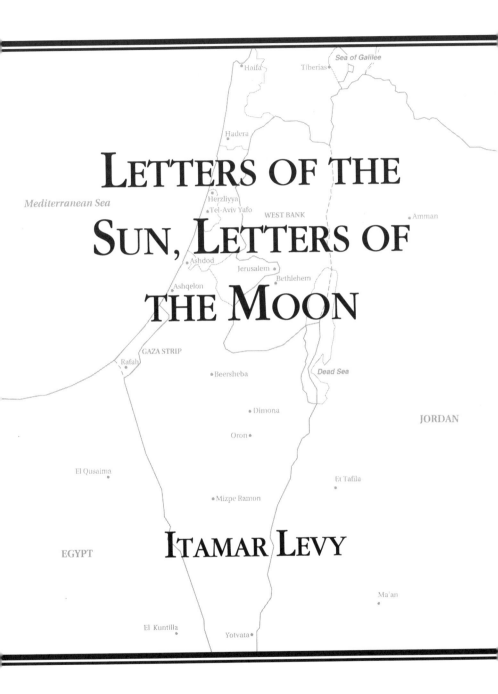

Letters of the Sun, Letters of the Moon

Itamar Levy

Itamar Levy was born in Tel Aviv in 1956. He studied theater at Tel Aviv University. Mr. Levy is a novelist, playwright, and radio scriptwriter. In addition, he worked on the editorial staff of the daily *Hadashot*.

Mr. Levy was awarded the Prime Minister's Prize for Literature. He is the author of four novels, a number of which have been translated into French, German, and Italian. The following selection is an excerpt from his most recent novel, *Letters of the Sun, Letters of the Moon*, a fantastical account of Arab life as seen through the eyes of a young Palestinian boy living on the West Bank.

Mr. Levy lives in Tel Aviv.

THE LETTER ALIF, أ

THE FIRST LETTER IN THE ALPHABET OF THE HOLY TONGUE

The night was one.* In the distance their voices rose with laughter and the music that never fades. The usual chattering was mingled with the sounds of women.

We made ourselves ready. One and all we examined our clothes and the equipment we had been given. I had been given Moshe Dayan.** With the General's insignia, with the black plastic eyepatch. And I was not the only Moshe Dayan. Ibrahim Nasrallah, my heroic friend, was also Moshe Dayan. And crazy Khaled Almajid, he too was Moshe Dayan, seven years old. Also Abd Ali, known as A.A., and Yusuf, and Walid. Among us were also Mickey Mouse, a sailor, a streetsweeper, a monster, a cowboy, cosmonauts, and soldiers. Many soldiers were there. Many identical witches. Many twin clowns. A great many Arabs. Like a military parade. Like a procession by the National Circus of Riga. Like a troop of pupils on the way home from school. Like the funeral of Ziyad, who was soon to die, a senseless death. There were many doctors among us. Many wounded men with plaster casts, with bandages, with painted-on blood stains. Many Moshe Dayans. Charlie Chaplin was there. A blue policeman holding the arm of a religious Jew from Jerusalem. A king came, a robber, a Japanese, Siamese twins joined at the shirt, noblemen, Napoleons, counts and knights, janitors and servants, and princesses, and dwarves, and drunks. One

---

*This selection is set in a Palestinian village on the West Bank.
**General Moshe Dayan—Israeli political and military leader.

William Tell. One Indian fakir. A youth who had turned himself into an old man, and an old man who had made himself young. One as the Angel of Death, another as a skeleton, and another who had turned into a demon with red horns, who had turned into Satan. Someone disguised as Pinocchio. Someone as Snow White. The sound of a multitude of clowns. The sound of a multitude.

Let no one say that these things never happened. Let no one say that the child Jaafar Omar Ismail Zakut is imagining things again. I saw it with my own eyes, the right one and the left one, how the first among us broke down the door of the sewing-shop of the African Ahmed Said Charles Latif, who had offered his three sewing machines and his four family members to sew faces for the enemy's festival of masks.* To sew Moshe Dayan, and Mickey Mouse, and sailors, and policemen, and soldiers. The son of the African traitor was with us too. Faiz Latif, who covered his black skin with charcoal and a straw skirt made by his mother, and dressed up as a cannibal.

The dirt and asphalt alley streamed between the houses. Silvery puddles of sewage decorated the dead village, multiplying the doors and windows and sky, and the children ashamed of being left out of our procession on its way toward the soldiers. Many paths run to the main artery, the street of shops and businesses paved by the army, veining the village like the palm of a grape leaf. Many paths and alleys run to the street, but they never succeed in meeting it. At first the enemy had stationed soldiers in all the alleys, to guard their passing motorcars. But we had repulsed them back to the main street, and within the hour they had closed off the entrances to the street with welded iron bars. The gates had smiled at us,

---

*This refers to Purim, a Jewish festival that commemorates the deliverance of the Jews of Persia from destruction by Haman, in celebration of which costumes are donned.

inviting us to throw stones through them at the yellow cars. As soon as we had, the enemy retaliated with woolly balls of barbed wire. They had laid down rusty oil barrels, one on top of the other. They had put up a giant fence to block the smooth, arcing stones that we flung at them. The wall was so high that the soldiers had had to stand on the roofs of red buses to tie the wire netting to the poles. First gates, then balls of barbed wire, then barrels, then road-blocks of boulders, then a giant fence. And after these a brick wall and steel netting twice as high so that any who climbed it, like my beloved, my brother, could touch the clouds and the stars.

With my own eyes, the light one and the dark one, I saw how the first among us cut through the twelve roadblocks protecting the main street and pushed the others through the holes, and there marshaled them into a column of fancy costumes and masks and grotesque disguises. High high on top stood the princes and the knights, and the rab-bits. Below them were the priests and the counts and the vampires. Under them the Scots and the witches, and at the bottom the Red Indians waited to lead the procession forward. Our main street is not a terraced avenue, nor a curving promenade winding down to the sea. Instead it resembles an abyss, a steep plunge. Instead, our whole vil-lage stands on its side, crooked in the front. The gray houses teeter as if testing their balance. The lampposts lean to the right and lean to the left. The trees are bent from birth. The animals are born with their forelegs slight-ly longer. The people with their foreheads close to the ground. The mountains topple over, and the hills, and the sewage froths and churns and sweeps down the alleys to the street of the shops. A man puts his shoes down next to his bed and in the morning finds them waiting for him at the door to the room.

The masked youths measured the street plunging into the abyss and found it to be 3,966 feet from its highest point, at the house of the barber Abu Tufik, to its lowest point, at the newspaper stand of the teacher Jaafar Husein Husein. After the stand came the camp. The enemy chose to pitch his tents there intentionally. None of us youths would dare cast stones at the soldiers and then clamber back up the terrible steep slope.

Everything needed to live sparingly exists on the main street of the shops. A grocery store, a barbershop, a newspaper stand, a tailor in his sweatshop—in other words the boot-licking African Ahmed Said Charles Latif—a pharmacy that became a cafe, and a tire store that would soon burn down because of the treachery of the owner. A long time ago the street was buzzing with trade. Twenty-nine shops operated and made a profit. One man sold shoes for ornamental purposes only; one, books for study and books for enjoyment; and one, sweetmeats deserving a stall of their own. Today the street is a patchwork of businesses shut down behind their iron curtains. Their owners have chosen to spend the years of curfew in their homes. Some of them chose to go and work in the ice cream factory for the prince of merchants, Sayyed Zakut, my esteemed father, who conducts most of his business with the help of the prayer books. The esteemed ice cream manufacturer opens the Holy Book with his eyes closed, sets his fat finger on the lines, and says: "Let us pray, let our prayers be answered. The Holy Book commands and instructs me to do so-and-so!"

If only I had the Koran with me, I would open its pages, point a blind finger at one of its verses, and know by the first letter which of us was soon to die from the soldiers' bullets. I would know who it was who had been advancing on the village for several days now, his shape the shape of a cloud. Who was coming to us riding on wheels of dust. Who was coming closer and obliging me to concern myself with him, while the troops of clowns and knights and animals were silently rolling past the enemy's camp. The masked procession descended, and on the way I scanned the garbage of the street impaled by the wind on the crosses of the fence, in the hope that Allah would return my pages to me. The Arabic language primer, brought to me by my beloved, was missing the first eight pages.

In all the houses of the village the light is yellow in the rooms and weak. Only in the soldiers' camp is the light white. In all the houses of the village the light is weak, and the heat of the stove is weak, and the running of the water is weak, and the sound of the radio is weak, and the voices of the people are weak. As soon as the road became flooded with resplendent light, the leaders knew that the end of the descent had come, and they stopped outside the entrance to the camp. From the tents rose the voices of the army, and their laughter, and music, and the usual chatter, and the sounds of women. Group by group the adults divided the street between us. In a few hours the world would wake, the enemy would wake, and find us hiding behind costumes and masks so they would not recognize us. They would find us stationed in groups of two-legged cats, and butterflies, and the heroes of cartoons, and messengers from outer space, and Ramseses and Cleopatras, and strawberries, and carrots, and ducks, and zebras, and monkeys, and parrots, and a snake, and a wolf, and belly dancers, and priests.

The feet drummed their last steps and were still. Surrounded by several figures of General Dayan—including Ibrahim Nasrallah, the brother of Ibtisam, and crazy Khaled Almajid, and A.A., in other words Abd Ali, whose father is blind, and Yusuf, and Walid—I rested my elbow on the stones of the road, and I rested my ear on my hand. I thought of Ahmed Said Charles Latif. The thoughts turned into dreams, the dreams took on the semblance of reality, and I myself turned into the treacherous African tailor, whose father's father had once set out from Sudan for Mecca, lost his way, and ended up in our village. In my dream I sat in my car and chased the thieves who had stolen the fancy costumes. In my dream I drove slowly down the street of businesses, peeping into every alleyway, to seek out those who were hiding from me. In the end the masks surrounded me, held on to the steel and glass of the car, and began to shake me again and again, up and down, to and fro, until my whole belly shrank, until I fell dead on my steering wheel. A long hoot sounded, like the long beep of a resuscitation machine. In my death I saw my son, my friend Faiz Latif, standing helpless at one side of the picture, dressed up as an African, his tears white as he cried: "Why, Father?! Why?! Why are you called 'Charles'?!"

A string of shots pierced the black of the sky, startling my sleeping eyes, jolting the weapon of the sentry, who had noticed the mysterious figures standing in a silent demonstration opposite his post. Our leaders barked commands to the rear and threw their stones in the direction of the naked soldiers rushing out of the tents. The ranks shouted: "*Allah akbar! Allah akbar!*"* Those of us who could do so shed their outer forms and heaped them into little bonfires before they were caught by the enemy. The burning costumes and the soldiers' tear gas canisters bloomed flowers of smoke and filled the street. A chimney of smoke on this side and a chimney of smoke on that. Pillar after pillar. Arc after arc, opening into the mouth of a cave above our heads. High into the air rose the mist, then fell back toward me and kissed my mouth like the smoke of a cigarette.

Two seized hold of me. An officer and his helper. Attached to each other by a long cord, like a camel and its driver. The officer tore the General's insignia from me together with the eyepatch and flung them at my feet. The soldier's fingers felt my body and thrust into my pockets.

Allah Akbar—"God is great" in Arabic.

146

There were rings of blood on the street. The enemy ordered everyone who had been caught to advance toward "the pissing wall." As in the Debka dance*, we all held hands. I gave my hands to the others, the others gave me their hands, and we were all hand in hand. A band of beggars, a swarm of wasps, a coterie of kings, and a flock of fairies. Some as monkeys. Some as Superman. A thousand pirates. A thousand Moshe Dayans. Among the dancers I saw my beloved, my brother, spectacles of blood painted round his eyes.

For many years my father, my master, had attempted to subdue the stormy spirit of my brother. The best war against the Jew, in his opinion, was not one of stones and the *shabab***: It was us, the youth, but by developing our Palestinian economy. "The white piastre*** will help on the black day!" he would quote his wisdom. An ice cream business, my father argued, was good both for times of peace and for evil days. At the honored command of our master, my beloved was sent seven years ago to study refrigeration engineering in the foreign city of Riga. For seven accursed years he was away from us, and only now had he returned to contribute his experience to the struggle.

From here, from where I stand, I cannot tell which of us is which. Who is the bee, and who the robot, and who the scarecrow. I can only recognize the soldiers confiscating the papers of the masked youths. Among them bands of pirates, and bands of vampires, and a band of Greeks and Romans. Like the eyelid quick to shelter the eye against every harm, so God protects his believers and shelters them. No sooner did the berets advance to constrain my brother's skull-and-crossbones in white handcuffs and load him onto their car, than the tire store on the hill put

*Debka dance—traditional Arab dance.
**shabab—"youth" in Arabic. This term took on revolutionary meaning during the Intifada.
***piastre—currency used during the British Mandate period.

on a coat of black wool and attracted their attention. The army and the citizens mingled with each other and turned into a chorus. Out of the clouds of fire billowing from the windows of the shop and its door they pulled Ziyad Hafez Elkhatib, and he was a burned shadow. O Ziyad, O Ziyad, what kind of a senseless death did you choose for yourself? What made you slip away from the soldiers rounding us up and climb heavily up the hill on your crutches? Your real legs were shorter than the silver legs joined to your hands. What made you twist the dead half of your body on that pair of irons and advance like a skier between the puddles? Your face hidden beneath the pirate's mask was raised toward the tire store. My beloved did not linger to examine "The Shadow's" revenge; he took my hand and smuggled me back into the house.

A goat will remain a goat even if it sprouts wings. A man remains a man even if he disguises himself as Moshe Dayan. When I returned, the neighbors' dogs came out to greet me. My donkey smiled at me and laughed, he twisted his neck around me and chased away his friends so they would not bother me on my way to bed. Behind the walls the gate creaked ominously. The sound of threatening footsteps crushed the gravel on the path leading to the front door. Since I did not recognize those who were coming, since I did not know whom they were seeking, I opened the shutter of my room a crack and I saw:

THE LETTER BA, ﬚

WHICH IS THE SECOND LETTER IN THE HOLY ALPHABET, AND ITS NAME IS BA

In my thin exercise book I write. i. i. i. Write and look. Proudly I look. Many words, my brother told me, begin with the letter alif. Important words. i. i. i. All by myself I learn. *Ana, ana.* I. I is with alif, and father is with alif, and lion is with alif, and brother is with alif, and Allah begins with alif. Only for your sake, Allah, I am learning to write. Only for your sake, Allah, to read and to pray and to believe. I have already reached the second letter, bā. One day I will be able to read the slogans written in your honor on the walls.

Sometimes my imagination blurs. Sometimes I wander from thought to thought. There are some who call me a chatterbox or a liar. But all my words are the truth and can be proved. I do not make things up, nor invent stories, as some people say. In my exercise book my brother wrote my name, Jaafar Omar Ismail Zakut, and the name of my village, and the name of my honored father. In spite of my age, I do not know how to read and write, because of the closed schools. With the help of the primer my brother found, I devote a little time to myself and learn the letters of the Koran.

I already know what is permitted and what is forbidden. It is permitted to pray, it is permitted to fast, it is permitted to make the pilgrimage. It is forbidden to eat pork, forbidden to blaspheme, forbidden to murder, forbidden to earn interest on money. Wine is forbidden, and games of chance are forbidden, even though we play them every Thursday evening at Ali Abd Almajid's cafe. It is forbidden to violate the curfew. It is strictly, strictly forbidden to insult the soldiers. It is forbidden to go out to meet the cloud of dust that has been approaching us now for days. My father's salesman told us apprehensively about the whirlwind that is in the sky, and it is on its way here. Who is advancing toward the village and his shape is the shape of a curl? Who is coming to us riding on wheels of dust?

A father I have. And a grandfather of stone. And two brothers. The older of them, Sharif Arafat Zakut, whom I have never met in my life, works in the lands of the oil. The younger of them is my beloved, the juggler from Riga, who will be killed one day because of the soldiers. My mother died when I was born, and the mother of my father is Suad Mahmud Zakut the devourer. Out of respect for her and her needs, a divan bed was installed in the pantry. It is my duty to make sure that the mountains of food placed before her all day long do not disappear.

From the day that my brother Sharif set off on his travels nothing has been heard from him, nothing but rumors and rumors. No letter has come from him. No telegram has come from him. No postcard, and no food parcel. Not even one telephone call had been received, nothing but rumors and rumors. The lands of the oil are distant lands, farther than the deserts and the houses, higher than the trees. Year after year the pilgrims returned from Mecca and told of meeting him. Some claimed that he was driving an oil truck. Some claimed that he was operating an oil rig. Some had seen him descending solemnly from Mount Arafat.* No solid facts, nothing but rumors and rumors.

He has an ice cream factory, my master Zakut. Huge vats of pink liquid, and yellow liquid, and orange, and black, and brown. Inside each container a huge fan turns without stopping and creates a sucking and churning. Sometimes I stand on the tips of my shoes and peek inside them. They bubble and suck and churn. They are deep as wells, as chasms, as the pits gaping in the flesh of my Grandmother Zakut. They are a rainbow of colors. Sometimes I peek into the refrigeration rooms and storerooms. The workers inside are dressed as if for a snowstorm. With gloves, and thick coats, and woollen hats, and wind goggles, and special shoes. Like rows of bats, the different flavors hang upside down above my head on the production line.

Sayyed Zakut comes home from work in the ice cream factory. He puts on his striped gown, which to me is like

---

*Mount Arafat—granite hill 15 miles southeast of Mecca, an object of pilgrimage.

the robe of the prophets, and swaying forward and back-ward like a stately camel makes his way to the room of the books. There he settles himself sturdily on his knees, takes the holy Koran from the bottom shelf, and reads it as he leans on the glorious tower of cushions on his right. My honored father has many books. Higher books and lower books, proud books and humble books, encompassing in their multitudes his majestic and rooted kneeling. And when the master of the house lowers his forehead to the narrow carpet, and when he raises his hands to Mecca—neither lengthening nor shortening, but all in the neces-sary degree, in obedience to the rules of the ritual, in accordance with the traditions handed down in our blood—the members of the household hold their breath in admiration and fear and imitate his movements in their imagination.

"A white spot on the forehead of the horse does not guarantee victory in the race!" says Sayyed Zakut, citing a proverb whose meaning is not clear to us. All his business, as well as the running of the household, he conducts with the help of the Koran. When he is faced with an important decision—when he has to decide how to revenge himself on his rival Muhammed Mahmud Almajid, or how to punish one of his rebellious sons—he closes his eyes and opens the book of God at random. Saying "This Koran will guide me on the right path!" he lays his clean hand on the words, and it is they that determine his actions.

Apart from the room of the books there is also the great hall in which the head of the house receives his guests. Beyond the steps leading to the second floor is the kitchen. The kitchen has three doorways and four windows. The first doorway leads to the reception hall. The second door-way leads to the pantry in the backyard, where my grand-mother the devourer sleeps. The third entrance is a corridor that connects the house to the rooms of the younger generation and the bathroom and lavatory. The end of the corridor was closed off by the builders with wood and glass: A narrow bed and a little table were crammed behind them, and this was declared to be my room. From my window I see the wall of bushes. Above it rises the minaret of the muezzin and the smoke from my father's factory. Next to me is the room of my beloved, and the room of the absent Sharif, and the room of my grandfather Isam Hareb Zakut, who lives inside the rock. Who lives inside the lime.

Suad Mahmud Zakut, my grandmother, was twenty years old when her husband died. A painter of walls was my grandfather, and he died by drowning in his white-wash. Perhaps he never died at all. For in his room, for on his bed, for behind my walls, lies a huge rock of lime. A lump of plaster, in which he hides. Sometimes we place him opposite the window so he can look out on the street and breathe the fresh air. Sometimes we cover his limbs.

All her life long my grandmother eats, my grandmother chews, and sucks, and with a black tongue licks the remains from her fingers. I lay before her lettuce leaves. Spinach in all its forms. A soft-boiled egg, whose smell is of hell but whose taste is of paradise. Sardines in a tin, and sardines in a barrel, and fresh sardines from the fisherman's net. In order to impress her and help her pass the time pleasantly I display my knowledge before her. Here is the letter alif, i, and here is the letter ﺑ , which is the second letter in the holy alphabet, and its name is bā. While she rummages in her food, I spread out my war collection. In it is a purple soldier's beret, and a green beret, and a black one, and a red. In it is the magazine of a gun with three live bullets. In it is an army belt with a water canteen. In it is a field dressing. In it is a tin of battle rations, which I am keeping for my grandmother in the hour of need.

Before I began to study the language of the Messenger, I idled my hours away in games and amusement. My room was covered with objects that I stole from the army, and with weapons that I devised, such as poisoned arrows carved from fresh ice cream sticks. Now, since I have begun to teach myself, letter after letter, the letters of the one almighty God, since all my days are dedicated to reading and writing, my room has begun to empty of these toys. At the end of the corridor the builders built my room. Its breadth is greater than its length. I have an entrance made of wood and glass. I have a wall for my bed, and a wall for shelves, and a wall for my table, which is the wall of the window. Above my table my beloved wrote verses from the Koran, which I do not understand. Above my bed I hung the picture of the poetess Umm Kulthum, the imaginary lover of my master.

Translated from the Hebrew
by Dalya Bilu

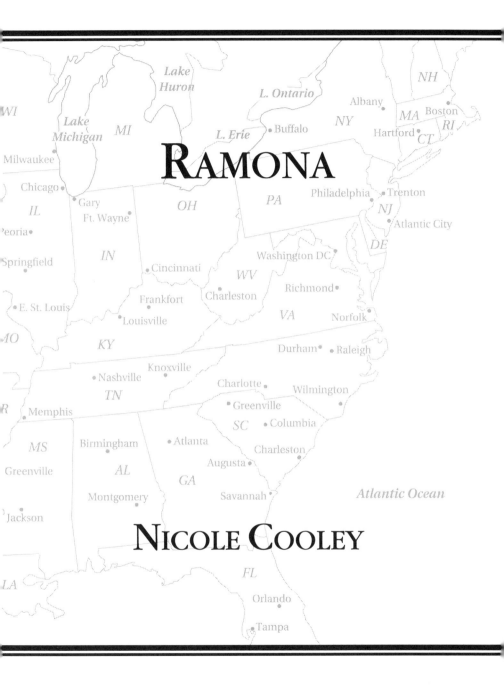

RAMONA

NICOLE COOLEY

Nicole Cooley was born in Iowa City, Iowa, in 1966 and grew up in New Orleans. She received a bachelor's degree in comparative literature from Brown University and a Master of Fine Arts degree in creative writing from the University of Iowa.

Ms. Cooley is the author of several short stories that have appeared in the *Iowa Review*, the *Mississippi Review*, and the forthcoming collection *Voices of the Exiled: A Generation Speaks for Itself*, among others. Her poetry has been published in a number of publications, including *Poetry*, *Southern Poetry Review*, and the *Seattle Review*. She is the recipient of a number of awards, including a Yaddo Corporation residency in 1992, and both a Ragdale Foundation residency and the *Ambergris* Annual Fiction Prize in 1993. She was awarded the 1994 "Discovery"/*The Nation* Poetry Award.

Ms. Cooley currently lives in Atlanta. She is completing her PhD in English at Emory University and working on a novel.

In April, when Ramona told everyone she was engaged to be married, she started carrying her grandmother's cocktail purse decorated with a pink fish and a velvet cut-up lemon. It was so sad, she said to her friends at school, that Jimmy Dell had moved to Lake Charles; it was almost as if he'd been drafted into the army. She wiped her eyes with tissues a lot, imitating her mother, like a woman in pain. "I might not see him again until I'm seventeen," she said. Everyone agreed that three years was a very long time. Her friends told her she was brave, but Ramona cried a lot that spring. Sometimes she thought she could taste salt at the back of her throat from her own tears. She didn't want anyone to think she was crying about her father.

The only person Ramona suspected did not believe her story about Jimmy Dell Roberts was Merilee Williams. At lunch, when Ramona told the other girls about the letters she was writing to Lake Charles, Merilee stood at the edge of the group with a bored expression and traced the toe of her shoe in the dust of the yard. Ramona had always wanted button-strap shoes. Last year, a rumor spread all over school that once, in the alley between St. Andrew's Church and the parish hall, Merilee let Jimmy Dell put his hand underneath her school skirt.

Ramona believed her situation might be improved by "the other woman" who was bad. She'd read about this kind of evil woman that men can't help loving in one of the magazines at her grandmother's house. Merilee didn't invite Ramona to her Mardi Gras party, and when Ramona came into homeroom in the morning, Merilee wrinkled her nose with distaste at Ramona's cocktail purse.

Merilee's mother drove a yellow convertible. Their family lived in a house with columns on the front porch and two crepe myrtle trees in the yard. When her mother picked her up after school, a little white powder-puff dog sat beside her on the front seat. Ramona took the bus to school or walked with her friend June. Her mother never let the cat, Mathilda, in the living room. Mathilda slept in Ramona's bedroom closet, on top of a stack of boxes of her father's clothes. "I don't want to see them," her mother said. "I never want to look at them again."

Ramona sat at the kitchen table and looked up all the words in Webster's Dictionary that began with Z. As she turned the pages, she twisted the two strands of pearls she wore with the bedjacket, her grandmother's, made of pink chenille. She wanted the jacket to show a curve in her chest, like the faint shadow she could see through June's school blouse. But June kept her arms folded across her front whenever boys were around. June's mother had told her she wasn't old enough to wear a bra.

Ramona touched the pearls to her lips, thinking of a picture in her English textbook called "Woman Preparing Her Toilette." In the painting, a woman sat at a dressing table, pearls circling her neck, a brush in her hand, watching her own reflection. Ramona imagined herself as that woman, elegant and alone, preparing herself to spend an evening with her lover. The textbook said this picture was hanging in the New Orleans Art Museum. Ramona had never been to New Orleans, although a bus going there stopped in Alexandria every afternoon.

"I'm just passing time till the mailman comes, hopefully with a letter from you know who," she told her mother, who had walked into the kitchen. Her mother lit a cigarette, running one hand through her hair, then looking at her fingers as if checking for strands that might have caught on her nails. In pictures taken when she was first married, her mother looked like a magazine model, and Ramona always offered to set her mother's hair to make it look the way it used to. Now her mother wore her blond hair short and uneven, with strands that fell into her eyes and over her forehead, unpinned. Ramona remembered how her grandmother used to come over every other week to wash her mother's hair with vinegar and lemon juice from a spray bottle to keep it very light.

After her father went away, Ramona's mother started smoking Luckies. "People are starting to talk," Ramona's grandmother said. "I don't care myself, but it'd be different if you were a widow." Ramona could think of only two widows in Alexandria. A rumor started a few years ago that one of them, Miss Millie LeBeau, had buried her husband in her own backyard on Galvez Street. Other people said Mr. LeBeau was still in the bedroom, dead on top of the oak frame bed.

Ramona touched the cigarette package that lay on the table between her and her mother and traced the red design. "You don't mind, do you?" she said, trying to be casual. "I think I'm having a fit for a cigarette." She didn't know exactly what a fit was, but she'd heard her grandmother talk about how her grandfather had them after the war. Ramona couldn't remember her grandfather acting strange, but she couldn't really remember him at all, as he'd died when she was in the first grade.

"You don't need to smoke. Who do you know who smokes at school?" Her mother didn't wait for an answer and picked up her cigarettes. "I'm going to lie down. If anything comes in the mail other than bills or magazine ads, bring it upstairs."

She knew her mother was probably going to stay upstairs for the rest of the afternoon. Sometimes she asked Ramona to soak a washrag in vinegar for her forehead, a remedy of Ramona's grandmother's, invented when she came to stay at the house in January. Above her mother's forehead, only the little pieces of short hair were bleached pale. Her face always looked damp. Ramona heard the radio music begin. In her mother's bedroom, faint music

159

was practically always playing. Sometimes her mother plugged up her ears with tissue when she lay on her bed, but she never turned off the radio.

Shutting the dictionary, Ramona began an article in the *Ladies' Home Journal*, "The Real Truth About Real Love." When the mailbox clanged, she counted to six as slowly as she could. Then she opened the door. She studied an ad for a Louisiana Sweepstakes offering a trip for two to Baton Rouge and a coupon for a free facial, which she decided to keep. Then a thin blue envelope stamped Kansas, with her father's writing on the front. This month, two postcards had come from Kansas, from Kansas City and Wichita, both the kinds of cards a person sends when he doesn't have anything to say. On the back of one, a typed description took up half of the message writing space. He seemed to sign his name bigger than usual.

"There are many long nights to get through," Ramona wrote in the little leatherbound book her father had given her, this year's birthday present, mailed from somewhere in Oklahoma; the mark across the stamp was blurred. Her mother opened the present for her. "What a ridiculous gift for a fourteen-year-old. Look at this, Ramona, your father has no sense of anything. He doesn't know anything about you." She started to laugh in a high voice that didn't sound like a person.

Her mother hid the book at the back of her own closet, and Ramona didn't see it for three months; then one day she found it under a pile of folded curtains. On the first page, she discovered an inscription she hadn't seen before—*To my baby whose thoughts are worth more than mine.* It was signed *Forrester*, not *Daddy*. The F was bigger than all the other letters. It would have been a good one for her autograph book, she thought, if she still collected autographs. Whenever she practiced this signature of her father's, the writing looked more like drawing than a name.

"I've been trying to have dreams about Jimmy Dell, but I can't get a vision of his face in my head," Ramona wrote. "I wish I had a picture. I know that if I saw a picture even for a second I could memorize his face." He had skipped school the day the yearbook photographer came, so there was a black square where his face should have been.

"He looks a little like Daddy," she wrote, and then she crossed that out. She made a picture of her father's face in her mind, sticking the features together till they locked into the image of a photograph, like jigsaw pieces. Her mother must have hidden all the real pictures. There was no camera in the house now.

In January, a few weeks before he left, Ramona and her father went to see a movie, "The Fall of the House of Usher." Right before they were supposed to leave, at seven o'clock, her mother said she had decided not to go. Ramona's father yelled at her, "You never want to go anywhere. You leave everything up to me." Ramona heard the kitchen tap turned on, running. Her mother always turned on the water to drown out voices. But she could still hear her father's words— "You'd never leave this house if I didn't make you." Her mother wasn't speaking. Maybe the faucet was her voice.

In the middle of the movie, her father leaned toward Ramona and asked, "Are you scared?" She said yes, a lie. The people on the screen weren't frightening. An old man in a black cape made her laugh out loud when he ran so close to the camera that his face filled the screen like a Halloween mask, all black and white, no sound. On the screen, everything was falling down. Statues, books, leaves, and finally the white diamond-shaped casket turned over. "The world is falling apart," Ramona's father whispered, but he didn't look at her; he stared straight ahead. "Look at that."

That night, Ramona had nightmares. She dreamed her

mother was buried alive. She'd seen a TV movie about that happening to a woman once.

"Did you get a letter from him yet?" June asked Ramona in English class. She now asked this question daily, and Ramona hoped June still believed her story about Jimmy Dell. She was afraid June would ask her about the wedding.

"Probably today," Ramona said. "This morning, my horoscope in the paper said I'd have good luck."

At the front of the room, Miss Lewis, who was taping a sheet to the blackboard, told the class they were going to see a movie. Some of the boys clapped. "Remember that grammar exercises 55-67 are still assigned for tomorrow," she said. "Written out."

Merilee leaned across the aisle toward Ramona. "You better close your legs when you sit like that," she whispered. "I can see your panties." Ramona glared at her and tucked the folds of her plaid skirt between her knees.

The movie was about orphanages in Romania, picking babies from a line of cribs. The voice-over explained that the children were eligible for private adoption. The children were for sale. Then a woman in a blue dress appeared, surrounded by boys and girls who seemed to be crouching in her skirts.

In "The Nutcracker" ballet, the show her father took her to every Christmas, the part Ramona liked best was in the last act when an old woman hid twelve children in her ruffled skirt. Suddenly, they all ran out from between her legs and turned somersaults and handsprings across the floor. The first time Ramona and her father went, he told her this was his favorite dance. "Is that their mother?" June asked Miss Lewis without raising her hand.

"That's the teacher," Miss Lewis said. "All the mothers are gone."

"They don't have any mothers," Merilee said, loud enough for the whole class to hear. Then she said, looking directly at June and Ramona, "Their mothers are dead, stupid."

Ramona looked down at the floor. She imagined Merilee and Jimmy Dell standing together in the alley between the church and the parish hall. She imagined Jimmy Dell touching Merilee's hair.

The next day, *Frankenstein* arrived from North Dakota. Ramona's father sent it in a brown manila envelope. "That's it," her mother said. "I'm taking it upstairs."

"She's just mad because he never sends her anything," Ramona told her grandmother, who had come over for the afternoon. "Even the postcards are addressed to me."

Inside the envelope with the book, he had sent a plastic-covered packet of licorice. Ramona sat on the back porch with her grandmother and tied the red licorice into twists to wrap around her fingers, comparing her grandmother's hand to her own.

Her grandmother wore all her rings even when she dipped her hands into soapy water in the sink. She had four silver rings, all from her husband. That winter, Ramona's mother had taken off her single ring, and a white band circled her finger where the diamond should be. She looked at her hand a lot, as if she were checking for stains along her fingers.

FACTS ABOUT MY FAMILY, Ramona headed the page in her leather book. She had to stop thinking about Jimmy Dell. The *Ladies' Home Journal* article had said that it was important to shift attention away from one's "preoccupation and situation with the loved one" and to "concentrate on other people." The woman who wrote the article was speaking from personal experience; her husband had disappeared. "Keep busy," the writer said, "crocheting granny-square afghans or baking bread." Ramona had never been interested in any form of knitting. Jimmy Dell had not written in the three months since he left. She set her pencil between her teeth and tried to remember.

1. *My grandmother owns ninety-eight pairs of shoes.*

This may or may not have been true. Ramona believed her grandmother about most things. Once she searched the closet in her grandmother's house to make sure. Shoe boxes were stacked along the floor and on top of clothes, all labeled with black writing—Blue kid, Yellow sandals, Brown leather pumps. Her grandmother said that at one time she had dresses to match them all.

2. *My parents went to Lafayette on their honeymoon.*

She had found a packet of pictures from this trip taken with an Instamatic camera—one of her mother standing on a raft at the edge of the river, one of her father at a crawfish boil, another of the two of them with their arms around each other. Ramona wondered who had taken that picture. They were sticking out their tongues. Her mother's hair was brushed back into a long ponytail. Ramona had never seen her face with that expression before.

3. *We are related to Jefferson Davis.*

Her father had told her that. Her mother said it wasn't true. "Everyone in Louisiana has the name Davis somewhere in their family," she said. "It doesn't mean a thing." In third grade, Ramona told her teacher that Jefferson Davis was her great-grandfather, and the principal of the school called her house. "I have never been so embarrassed," her mother said.

4. *My mother is getting smaller.*

Sometimes, when Ramona came into her mother's room, she found her asleep, or at least pretending to be asleep, on the very edge of the bed. With the sheet pulled up over her chin and her lips, she looked tiny and quiet, like Mathilda when she was hit by a car in the street in front of the house. For days afterward, the cat crawled around the house, making no noise, but the doctor said nothing was wrong. Mathilda was in a black despair, her father said.

5. *My father isn't coming back.*

*   *   *

Ramona started a letter to her father. She knew she had no address to send it to. Miss Berdeen was talking about the Louisiana Purchase in Social Studies class, pointing her stick to places on the big map at the front of the room. Ramona liked the blue-green color of the map, but she couldn't pay attention. She remembered her grandmother's telling her how wandering Spanish men had invaded New Orleans. Her grandfather was Cuban, and her grandmother had developed a deep hatred of anything having to do with Spain, Mexico, or any other Spanish-speaking country. "He left the family right after your mother was born," she always told Ramona. "I had to work in a soup factory to get money to keep the house, and then I took in other people's children from the Lake Charles Children's Home. It was a terrible time." Her grandfather had come back one year later, and then he disappeared after the next daughter was born. "That was his pattern," her grandmother said. "That was what he did. But he came back every time; he always came back in the end." She shook her head.

After Ramona's father went away, her grandmother said, "And they aren't even related." She sat at the kitchen table and Ramona's mother tore up strips of washrags and nodded at her. She didn't say whether or not she thought it was true.

The bell rang and Ramona crumpled up the piece of notebook paper. She hadn't written a single word.

The afternoon he left, Ramona walked downtown. Whenever her parents fought, her father took the streetcar downtown; he always went alone. He'd go downtown, and her mother would run upstairs and close the bedroom door. By midnight, he was always back, and Ramona waited up for him, waited to hear the bang of the front door and the click of the lock as he came inside.

That afternoon, she knew she couldn't stay in the house

with her mother. She listened to the stutter of gravel in the driveway as the car pulled off from the house, like the noise the Senior boys made with their cars to show how fast they could drive away from school at the end of the day. Ramona waited for that sound, but she didn't watch the car turn the corner.

"I can't stay here anymore," was all he said. He said it to her mother. Ramona stood in the space between the dining-room french doors and listened, hoping no one could hear her breathing. She thought of how if she were Mathilda she would be very quiet in her hiding place and then jump out between her parents and then her father would laugh and pick her up and forget about the idea of leaving the house. But instead, she hid there, behind the door curtains, with one hand covering her mouth and her finger in her ear in case she decided she didn't want to hear anymore.

Her father wasn't saying anything. Ramona heard him pulling a suitcase out from under the bed and then the bathroom water running. Ramona imagined her mother lowering her face into the basin of water, all filled up. Maybe she was crying. Maybe she just wanted to drown out all the sounds.

On the way downtown, a yellow car drove down the middle of River Road, and Ramona hid from the glare of the lights. It was raining. She was scared that someone from school would see her. Her father always told her not to go downtown alone, but the mannequins in the store windows were the only people that scared her. They had smooth faces with painted eyes and no noses. That afternoon, she watched the mannequins in the big front windows of *Maison Blanche*. It was Sunday; no one was out. She tried to imagine where her father would go. Once before, he had left and driven to New Orleans, spent the night at the airport and come straight back.

*　　*　　*

When Ramona had her tonsils taken out three years ago, her father went with her to the hospital. Before the operation, he sat in the room and showed her a trick. He invented a game for them to play—he folded paper in half and drew part of a picture that she couldn't see. Next, she drew. Then he flattened out the paper to see what they had made together. One time, they drew a dragonfly with almost perfect wings.

Ramona lay in the hospital bed and felt very tired. She could smell the gas they told her they'd give her to make her sleep, although the nurse hadn't come in yet. She felt the taste of it in the room. Before she finally fell asleep, she thought she heard her father's voice, talking about the insect on the piece of paper. "See, look, Ramona, our minds work the same way." He never mentioned this again, and she was never sure if she had made it up or not.

The night before he left for Lake Charles, she told this story to Jimmy Dell. She had never talked to him about her father before, and she wasn't exactly sure why she was telling him now.

"Hey, Ramona, I have to go," he said, after she told him the story, "My mom says it's time for supper."

Ramona didn't believe him, but she hung up the phone. There was a lightness inside her then, as if there was too much silence in the room. She told herself that she was already missing Jimmy Dell.

The day after Ramona went out with Jimmy Dell, she watched him all morning in school and pretended she wasn't waiting for him to talk to her. In Social Studies class, she wrote a note to June on the back of the chapter test on Wanderers, Explorers and Conquerors of the South. *"Jimmy and I had a wonderful time,"* she wrote quickly. She could feel June watching her. *"We talked for a long time in the park. He was wearing his green baseball jacket and he looked perfect."* She slid the piece of paper under the toe of her shoe across the floor to June, who read it and smiled with approval. June mouthed the question, "Did he kiss you?" Ramona pretended not to see.

At recess, June followed Ramona out to the yard. "There he is," June said, squeezing Ramona's arm. He was playing kickball. "He's wearing the jacket."

"Well, I guess he didn't see me." Ramona was trying to think of a reason to go home for the rest of the day. "June, I've got to run home to check on my mother. She's been kind of sick. I'll see you this afternoon."

Ramona ran all the way down Galvez Street, and when she got to her house, the kitchen window was open. Ramona stood on a brick in the grass and looked in the window before she opened the door. Her mother was bent over the table; only the back of her neck showed. Her mother might have been sewing or concentrating on something very small with her hands. But she wore a dress that Ramona thought had once belonged to her grandmother, and her back was shaking.

Her mother made a sound. Ramona stepped back from the window, putting her hands over her ears. It was like the screech of the cat right before Dr. Connors put her to sleep for the first time. Mathilda hadn't died; the doctor said she was resilient, but she would live a life of misery. That noise, her father had said, was the most horrible sound in the world. Her father let Mathilda come home with them again.

On the evening of her first and only date with Jimmy Dell, Ramona put on her favorite outfit, the one her father bought her for Christmas, her Neapolitan ice cream dress. He called it that because the dress had big colored stripes down the front. Her mother hated it; she made a face every time Ramona wore it, and once Ramona overheard her mother telling her father that he had no idea of taste if he would pick out such a sick-looking pink color.

Ramona watched *I Love Lucy* as she brushed her hair. Ricky and Lucy were fighting, and then Lucy started to cry, the way she always did, screwing up her face with her mouth open wide. Ramona practiced this expression in the mirror. She rolled her hair with Tropicana cans, spreading gel on her fingers to wet the curls. The pink in the jar matched the cloth of her dress, which was spread out on the bed and pressed by her grandmother, still steam-damp. She set out the things she'd need for the evening: her cocktail purse, a lipstick of her grandmother's, and the plastic picture wallet her father sent her from Cullman with ALABAMA stamped on it in blue letters. Her mother had told her the wallet was tacky too, but her grandmother called it "a conversation piece." Ramona told the girls at school that Jimmy Dell gave it to her. She figured no one would ever know that wasn't true.

She sprayed her mother's Shalimar all over her body, even a little between her toes. *Vogue* magazine said scent rises from the feet. Except for the low hum of her mother's radio, the house was quiet.

"I feel too keyed up to eat," Ramona told her grandmother, who had come over for the evening. "I really couldn't put anything in my mouth." But her grandmother offered chocolate mint ice cream and root beer, so Ramona poured herself a glass of soda with a couple of spoons of ice cream. "This might settle my stomach. I'll drink it slowly."

"Your mother is staying upstairs tonight," her grandmother said, with her back toward Ramona. "She has one of those headaches. You know how they make her tired."

Ramona rinsed the glass in the sink and smoothed some dishwashing liquid in her palms. She looked at her grandmother's back. "Can I go up and tell her goodnight?"

"You can talk to her tomorrow. She's probably asleep." Ramona nodded. Her hands felt sticky. She wondered if she should paint her fingernails. "I know you wouldn't mean to upset her, but she isn't feeling well today."

*   *   *

Ramona and Jimmy Dell stand on the top of the church, in the bell tower. St. Andrew's Church is the tallest building in Alexandria. Ramona has always been scared of it. Her father used to tell her that a man with one arm lived in the top of the tower. "I want to see the view," Jimmy Dell had said. "Let's go up and see the sky." Ramona has never been up to the top before, up the creaky wooden stairs, but Jimmy takes her hand and tells her where to step. Some of the stairs are missing.

At the top, it is so dark that all Ramona can see is the green glint of Jimmy's eyes, like the eyes of a cat. When he moves his hand to the little front buttons of her dress, she nearly screams, but she tells herself to stand very still. She waits for it to be over. She tries to hold her breath. She tries to count to twenty in French but can't remember the word for sixteen. His fingers are damp on her bare skin. She closes her eyes. He whispers something in her ear, but she can't be sure of what he's saying. He touches the waistband of her dress where the blouse and skirt button together.

Jimmy Dell walks Ramona to the corner two blocks away from her house, the halfway point between where they each live. On the way, he doesn't talk, but he keeps touching her back through the Neapolitan dress as if he wants to find the mark his fingers have already made on her skin.

When she gets home, she starts to cry and doesn't stop till the hall clock strikes three. Then she sees that her mother is not going to come in and see what's wrong. Ramona can't hear the radio through the wall. She waits for a long time, remembering how her grandmother came to stay up all night with her mother the night after her father left. But *left* is not the right word. What she wants to say is *disappeared* because that sounds more like a mystery book or the beginning of a fairy tale.

Glossary

ABT—American Ballet Theatre
advent—a coming or arrival
adagio—a movement or piece performed at a slow tempo
aflutter—in a state of excitement or confusion
aloof—at a distance; reserved or indifferent
baleful—deadly in influence, cynical, ominous
balustrade—a railing supported by small posts, as on a staircase
barbel—type of European fish
barre—a long round sectioned rail mounted horizontally and
    used by dancers in class for balance
bejeweled—covered or decorated with jewels
beringed—having rings on one's fingers
black tie—formal evening dress
bolge—pits in hell; in Dante's *Inferno*, the ten evil pouches
    within the Eighth Circle of Hell
bourée—a series of very fast little steps done with the feet close
    together
British Mandate—period preceding establishment of state of
    Israel during which Britain ruled the territory, 1920-1948
cambre—in ballet, an arching of the back, usually with arms
    overhead
cassava—any of several tropical plants cultivated for their
    edible tuberous roots
catamaran—ship with twin hulls, side by side
cherub—a celestial being, often represented as a rosy-faced
    child with wings
cistern—a large tank or building used to collect or store water
consignment—a shipment of goods sent to a dealer for sale
coterie—a group of people who associate closely because of
    common interests, etc.
creel—basket made of wicker or other material for holding fish,
    lobsters etc.
demiurge—a supernatural being who created the world
disinter—to remove a body from a grave or tomb
evocative—tending to call forth or summon a reaction
fatback—fat and fat meat from the upper part of a side of pork
ford—place where a river is shallow enough to cross by wading

171

fouetté—the whipping of the free leg to the side and to
the knee while turning continously on the standing leg
fuselage—the complete central structure to which the wing, tail
surfaces, and engines are attached on an airplane
giddy—dizzy; frivolous and lighthearted
gingham—cotton cloth of two or more colors, usually stripes or
checks
hamstring—either of two tendons at the rear hollow of the
human knee
hauteur—haughty manner or spirit
hitch—to move roughly or jerkily
kaleidoscopic—constantly changing color or pattern
Koran—the sacred book of Islam which is believed to contain
revelations made to Mohammed by Allah
leotard—a knit body suit used in dance and many sports
leucoma—a dense white opacity of the cornea
marl—a crumbly earthy deposit of clay and calcium carbonate
minaret—a tall slender tower attached to a mosque from
which the muezzin calls the people to prayer
misappropriate—to put something to wrong use
moraine—a deposit of boulders, gravel, sand, and clay left on
the ground by a glacier
muezzin—in Muslim regions, a crier who calls the people to
prayer five times a day
node—a knot, protuberance, or knob
ominous—threatening or sinister
partisan—a member of a party of light or irregular troops
engaged in harassing an enemy; guerrilla
pell-mell—in a jumbled, confused manner
pilgrimage—a journey, especially a long one, made to some
sacred place as an act of devotion
pirouette—a whirling about on one foot on the points of one's
toes
plié—a movement in which the knees are bent while the back is
held straight
pointe—the tip of the toe
ponderosa—a large pine tree of North America

porridge—cooked crushed oatmeal

port de bras—the various positions or movements of the arms
in ballet

primer—an elementary textbook for reading

proscenium—in a theater, the arch and curtain separating the
stage from the audience

pupal shuck—the shell of an insect larva

redoubt—an independent military structure built inside or
outside a fortification for defense; a stronghold

regal—royal; stately; splendid

relevée—rising of the body from flat foot to half pointe or full
pointe

resplendent—shining brilliantly; gleaming

retribution—punishment for evil done or reward for good done

rheumy—having a watery discharge from the eyes or nose

salvo—a discharge of firearms at the same time or in regular
succession

sardonic—sarcastic, cynical, contemptous

sodden—soaked with moisture; heavy, lumpy, or soggy

spot—fixing eyes on a point to control turns in ballet

stalwart—strong and brave

steely—like steel, as in coldness or hardness

talisman—amulet or charm

toque—a brimless close-fitting hat for women, in any of several
shapes

torrid—oppressively hot, parching, or burning; passionate or
ardent

tourmaline—a crystalline mineral

tribulation—great misery or distress

tulle—a thin fine netlike cloth

vagaries—odd, eccentric, or unexpected actions

zander—pike or perch

Further Reading

Alcott, Louisa May. *Little Women*. New York: Tor Books, 1994. Fiction: Saga of the four March sisters in Civil War New England.

Angelou, Maya. *I Know Why the Caged Bird Sings*. New York: Bantam Books, 1991. Nonfiction: Autobiography of the poet and writer.

Brontë, Charlotte. Jane Eyre. New York: Puffin Books, 1992. Fiction: A 19th-century classic.

Buck, Pearl. *The Good Earth*. New York: Pocket Books, 1991. Fiction: The saga of one family's life in China.

Carroll, Lewis. *Alice in Wonderland*. Cutchogue, New York: Buccaneer Books, 1981. Fiction: Classic novel of a young girl's coming of age in Wonderland.

Dickens, Charles. *Oliver Twist*. New York: Norton Critical Editions, 1992. Fiction: Classic novel about social injustice, including child abuse, in the 19th century.

Dostoevsky, Fyodor. *The Brothers Karamazov*. New York: Viking Penguin, 1982. Fiction: Four young brothers driven by passion murder their father.

Dumas, Alexandre. *The Three Musketeers*. New York: Penguin Classic, 1982. Fiction: The adventures of young French men struggling to preserve the honor of their queen.

Esquivel, Laura. *Like Water for Chocolate*. New York: Doubleday, 1993. Fiction: A young Mexican girl struggles with her position in her family.

Flagg, Fannie. *Fried Green Tomatoes at the Whistle Stop Café*. New York: McGraw, 1989. Fiction: Story of the enduring friendship between two young women in the South.

Forster, E.M. *The Longest Journey*. Cutchogue, New York: Buccaneer Books, 1989. Fiction: The story of two half brothers contrasts a zest for life with public school stuffiness.

Golding, William. *Lord of the Flies.* Cutchogue, New York: Buccaneer Books, 1992. Fiction: School boys marooned on a desert island revert to primitive savagery and superstition.

Gordimer, Nadine. *Burger's Daughter.* New York: Viking Penguin, 1980. Fiction: A young woman's evolving identity in South Africa.

Hale, Janet Campbell. *Bloodlines: Odyssey of a Native Daughter.* New York: Harper Perennial, 1993. Nonfiction: Autobiography of the Native American writer.

Kipling, Rudyard. *The Jungle Books.* New York: Viking Penguin, 1990. Fiction: A collection of stories including the saga of the lost boy Mowgli and his animal brothers and sisters.

Knowles, John. *A Separate Peace.* New York: Bantam Books, 1985. Fiction: A boy's coming of age at a New England boarding school and a fatal incident .

Kogawa, Joy. *Obasan.* New York: Doubleday, 1994. Fiction: Story of a Japanese family in a wartime internment camp in the United States.

Lee, Gus. *China Boy.* New York: Plume Penguin, 1994. A Chinese-American boy is unprepared for life on the streets of San Francisco.

Lee, Harper. *To Kill a Mockingbird.* New York: Warner Books, 1988. Fiction: A novel about racism, justice, and growing up in the South.

McCarthy, Mary. *The Group.* Cutchogue, New York: Buccaneer Books, 1991. Nonfiction: The story of eight Vassar women of the class of 1933.

Potok, Chaim. *The Chosen.* New York: Fawcett, 1987. Fiction: A young man struggles with his desire to lead a somewhat secular life and his strict orthodox Jewish upbringing.

Salinger, J.D. *The Catcher in the Rye.* New York: Fawcett, 1987. Fiction: Young Holden Caulfield faces the trials and tribulations of adolescence.

Simpson, Mona. *Anywhere But Here*. New York: Borzoi Books, 1986. Fiction: Examines a daughter's relationship with her mother.

Twain, Mark. *The Adventures of Huckleberry Finn*. New York: Tor Books, 1989. Fiction: The adventures of a young boy growing up in the South.

Index